THE 250
PERSONAL FINANCE
QUESTIONS EVERYONE SHOULD ASK

Peter Sander, M.B.A.

Adams Media
Avon, Massachusetts

Published by
Adams Media, an F+W Publications Company
57 Littlefield Street, Avon, MA 02322. U.S.A.
www.adamsmedia.com

ISBN: 1-59337-352-X

Printed in Canada.

J   I   H   G   F   E   D   C   B   A

Library of Congress Cataloging-in-Publication Data
Sander, Peter J.
The 250 personal finance questions everyone should ask / Peter Sander.
p.   cm.
Includes indexes.
ISBN 1-59337-352-X
1. Finance, Personal—Examinations, questions, etc. 2. Investments—Examinations, questions, etc. I. Title: Two hundred fifty personal finance questions everyone should ask.
II. Title: Personal finance questions everyone should ask. III. Title.

HG179.S26 2005
332.024—dc22

2005011198

This publication is designed to provide accurate and authoritative information with regard to the subject matter covered. It is sold with the understanding that the publisher is not engaged in rendering legal, accounting, or other professional advice. If legal advice or other expert assistance is required, the services of a competent professional person should be sought.

—From a *Declaration of Principles* jointly adopted by a
Committee of the American Bar Association and a
Committee of Publishers and Associations

Many of the designations used by manufacturers and sellers to distinguish their products are claimed as trademarks. Where those designations appear in this book and Adams Media was aware of a trademark claim, the designations have been printed with initial capital letters.

Interior layout and design by Electronic Publishing Services, Inc. (Tennessee)

This book is available at quantity discounts for bulk purchases.
For information, call 1-800-872-5627.

CONTENTS

INTRODUCTION

As the "ought" decade (2000–2009) unfolds, people are confronted with ever more critical and ever more complex management of their personal finances. As people change jobs, financial guarantees like pensions disappear. As financial markets become more uncertain, as home prices, health care, and tuition costs skyrocket, and the complex tangle of tax laws evolves, there is more to worry about. Are the solutions simple and straightforward? Hardly. How much money will you need in five years? Twenty years? To support a thirty-year retirement? To cover the possibilities of disability and unforeseen health problems?

Most people can't figure out what they need next week or month, let alone twenty years from now. Meeting today's needs and wants is so consuming of their time and money that there is little left over for tomorrow. The reality is this: It takes considerable energy, foresight, discipline, contingency planning, and a certain amount of good fortune to make your finances work to achieve your future goals. It requires a certain amount of professional skill to quantify and manage your personal finances.

Many people choose to leave the professional skill part to others—financial advisors, CPAs, stockbrokers, insurance agents, and the like. While this "leave the driving to us" model works for some, it is very dangerous in other circumstances. Financial professionals have to make money, and the harsh reality is that most make their money by selling something—insurance, securities, mutual funds, mortgages, and tax services. Can you get a complete, unbiased, and actionable financial strategy from these professionals? Yes, sometimes. But in the same way that it helps to know about cars before talking to a car salesperson or that it helps to know about paint before talking to a housepainter, so it follows that it also helps to know something about personal finance before talking to a financial professional. Otherwise, you may get something that meets their needs more than your own needs, and it rapidly goes downhill from there.

So today's savvy shoppers gather up information before buying a car. They visit manufacturer Web sites, automotive portals like Autobytel.com, *Kelley Blue Book, Car and Driver*, and so forth. They look at pictures, features, prices, dealer costs, repair data, and testimonials from other owners. Do these resources make the decision? Hardly. But along the way, they collect some key facts and impressions. More importantly, they *learn what questions to ask*. They can separate the jargon from the realities, and they are able to understand the facts and numbers well enough to decide.

Whether you are an individual or the head of a family, you are the chairman and CEO of your own financial destiny. Regarding your personal finances, you may choose to do it all yourself, delegate it all to others, or some combination of the two. Regardless, you'll need to arm yourself with the basics—the questions and at least some of the answers—to proceed. *The 250 Personal Finance Questions Everyone Should Ask* brings you a structured list of questions and answers covering all aspects of personal financial planning. The questions are designed to help you learn important facts and concepts about personal finance. In some cases, they may be used in direct conversation or to design the questions you might ask of a financial professional. Questions range from the strategic and conceptual "why" questions to the more tactical and precise "how" questions about specific financial tools.

The first group of these 250 questions covers personal finance as a broad topic. Next is a large body of questions covering daily personal finances—the management of income, spending, saving, budgeting, banking, and credit. From there, questions move to the more complex and subjective areas of financial planning. Topics include the achievement of financial goals such as college and retirement and the successful building of wealth to achieve these desired ends. The next set of questions covers external forces affecting the achievement of these goals—risk and taxes—that can sink your plans unless navigated successfully. In the last set of questions, the topic of managing assets when you can't—estate planning—is addressed.

PART 1

Managing Money

Chapter 1

PERSONAL FINANCE BASICS

The term "personal finance" makes the blood of many run cold. Uh-oh, here it comes. Too much month left at the end of my money. Not enough saved for retirement or college. Eight thousand dollars of debt on my credit card and growing. Budgets. Saving. Tax rules so complicated that even the enforcers don't understand them. The stock market, that emotional beast that ate so many for lunch in 2000–03. Insurance policies and contracts so complex that you hardly understand the reader-friendly version. Charts and graphs. The complex mathematical mysteries of compounding, making money worth more or less depending on time, an Einsteinian concept that might cause the genius himself to shake his head in confusion.

The truth is, unless you were raised in a firmly financially conscious household (and most of us weren't), most of the topics covered by personal finance represent scary, unfamiliar territory. Dealing with finances is, in two ways, a date with the devil. First, for most it uncovers the consequences and scary realities of what happens when you don't have enough money. Second, many of the solutions require that dreaded confrontation with the bank officer, insurance agent, stockbroker, or accountant, an encounter where you struggle to keep up with what they say and then somehow feel compelled to make a decision after listening to half an hour of incomprehensible stuff.

This chapter, containing the first 10 of the 250 questions, serves one of the main objectives of this book: to get you comfortable with the basic elements and philosophy of personal finance and financial planning. With this perspective, it should become easier to move forward.

Question 1: **What is personal finance?**

Boiled down, *personal finance* is nothing more than the management of your financial resources to meet your needs and achieve your desired goals. It is *personal;* that is, it's about you, your family, and your household. It is *finance;* that is, it concerns *money*—that which you have, that which you will have, and that which you need. It does not concern things—things are what you buy with money. It concerns how money is *acquired, stored,* and *used.*

The happy phrase "make it, spend it, keep it, grow it" summarizes the four major quadrants of personal finance. Personal finance requires attention to all four aspects in balance. Making money accomplishes little if it is spent frivolously. Consuming more than one produces is not viable in the long term. A household that makes and spends but doesn't save will achieve immediate gratification but will be caught short at some point in the future. A household that makes it, spends it, and manages to save some is on the right track but without growing it may fall short of achieving goals.

Personal finance involves planning both for today and for the future. The today part is managing current income, expenses, and savings. Planning covers aspirational goals and the many what-ifs of life.

The quadrant model of personal finance popularized by Robert T. Kiyosaki's *Rich Dad, Poor Dad* series is a good reference. The four quadrants are Income, Expenses, Assets, and Liabilities. The difference between Income and Expenses (net savings) builds

Assets (good) or Debt (bad). The difference between Assets and Liabilities is Net Worth, which, of course, is good if positive and bad if negative.

Personal finance essentially comes down to managing the four quadrants of your financial life.

Question 2: **Why is personal finance so important?**

Life's goals—and the means for achieving them—have become more complex and at the same time less stable. Jobs and careers, employee benefits, and costs of vital goods and services like homes, health care, and college education are changing ever more rapidly. Financial markets are less predictable, and pensions and even government entitlements, like Social Security, are less dependable as long-term fallbacks. We are literally bombarded with promotions to buy or finance something every day. The bottom line: Income and expenses have both become more volatile for the average citizen, and against that backdrop, people are living longer and have more ambitious aspirations. More careful management and planning are necessary to make sure it all works out right.

Question 3: **What personal character traits are required for financial success?**

Granted, it takes more than character traits to be financially successful—it takes hard work, some degree of knowledge, and at least a little luck. Beyond the basics, three character traits repeatedly emerge among financially successful people:

1. *Awareness.* To get where you're going, the first step is to know where you are. Financially aware people keep track of their current finances, including how much they get, where it all goes, and how much they have. They track the impact of large and small actions in their finances. They know how much they have in their pocket, what's on their credit cards, what's in the bank, what their investments are worth, and so forth. They

know the important parts of their financial plan, like their monthly budget, and how they are doing against them—not to the penny, that level of detail is unnecessary, but within a useful ballpark range.

2. *Commitment*—the ability and willingness to carry out the financial plan—follows awareness. Commitment must be universal in households; it doesn't work if only one family member is financially prudent.

3. *Control.* Control, in this sense, derives from commitment. It is the ability to control impulses, to make decisions with the big picture in mind, and to avoid temptations.

Successful personal finance requires a combination of all three traits. Any individual or family starting out should first take inventory of these traits, revisit them once in a while, and put proper rewards in place to reinforce their importance.

Question 4: **Regarding our finances, what can and what should we do ourselves?**

Personal finance can be a skill-intensive and time-consuming activity. The answer to this question really depends on your own priorities and willingness to invest time to learn and plan finances. Most people spend at least a few hours each week managing routine household income and expenses. The opportunity to outsource personal finance really enters with *financial planning*—that is, planning for college, retirement, taxes, and managing wealth to achieve goals.

When remodeling a house, anybody can be a "do-it-yourselfer." However, the process may be time-consuming and frustrating, and the outcome may not be what you had in mind—so you may decide to hire a contractor. Financial planning presents a similar choice. Many people choose to outsource, recognizing the loss of control and (usually) increased cost, but they make the tradeoff consciously. Still many more employ a mix—some "do-it-yourself" and some professionally managed, as with mutual funds. Unlike the remodeling project, the mix can be adjusted over time. But like the remodeling project, it can cost a lot to fix a bad job, and you as the owner must still take overall responsibility for the project.

Question 5: **Where should I/we get started?**

For many, getting started is one of the toughest assignments. People get used to a certain lifestyle. Then, confronted with the need (or desire) to improve their finances, they dread the necessary lifestyle changes. Habit changes and control issues between family members create tension and make it still harder to get started.

Experience proves it's best to start with a clear assessment of your current financial position—income, expenses, assets, and debt—almost like a company preparing year-end financial statements. Figure out where your income goes—the nature, frequency, and amount of each expense. It's okay—actually better—to group expenses into categories (e.g., Miscellaneous Personal) than to track down every $3.46 spent for a Starbucks latte. This thorough examination of past events to determine cause is called *financial forensics*. Count all assets and liabilities to determine net worth, and most of all, be honest.

The next step is to identify, quantify, and prioritize goals—things such as future home purchases, college education, retirement, vacations, and other aspirations. Then (and possibly with professional help) measure where you are today toward achievement of those goals, and the process is under way. Particularly for families, it works best if everybody works on this together, mainly to build the awareness, commitment, and control required to pull it off. Periodic review meetings support the process, and with a little success and reward mixed in, these sessions become part of the family entertainment repertoire.

Question 6: **Why do people fail financially, and how can it be avoided?**

The reasons for failure are many and varied, but most boil down to a lack of one or several of the following traits: awareness, commitment, and control. Simply writing checks or flashing the ATM card with no regard to where you are will bust a plan—if there was one in place to begin with. Many people spend too much, enjoying a standard of living possible in the short term—though often only with infusions of debt—but unsustainable in the long term. The problem is that they haven't even stopped to think about the long term! They have no awareness, and without awareness, commitment and control are impossible. It becomes a vicious cycle; once they get used to the standard of living, the long-term shortfall gets bigger and bigger. They become more reluctant to "face the music," and awareness, commitment, and control are further put off, and so on.

Question 7: **What should my net worth be?**

Net worth—what you own minus what you owe—is the primary financial engine driving the achievement of financial goals and, ultimately, your future standard of living. Why? Because as you get older, you produce less income by working, ultimately relying on income generated by your assets, plus government entitlements like Social Security, to live. Obviously, your net worth should be as high as possible, and the true amount of net worth needed is geared to your own personal goals and chosen lifestyle.

A useful and specific benchmark comes from researchers Thomas Stanley and William Danko and their seminal work *The Millionaire Next Door* (Longstreet, 1996). Stanley and Danko found that average net worth for the households they researched was a function of income and age and that it amounted to a person's Age times the Annual Income, all divided by 10. So if you're forty-five years old and have an annual income of $50,000, your net worth should be $225,000 [(45 × $50,000)/10]. If your net worth is more than twice this figure ($450,000), you are a Prodigious Accumulator of Wealth (PAW), and if your net worth is less than half ($122,500), you are an Under-accumulator of Wealth (UAW).

So get out your calculator, add up your assets and debts (including house, retirement plans, insurance policies, etc.), and figure out where you stand! Are you a PAW, UAW, or somewhere in between? The Stanley/Danko benchmark is a good place to start for setting financial goals.

Question 8: **I've heard a lot about the power of compounding. In plain English, what is it, how does it work, and why is it so important?**

Compounding is the mathematical miracle adding so much to your financial potential if handled properly. Compounding boils down to this: When assets earn a return (interest, dividends, growth) and that return is left on the table, not only do the original assets continue to earn return, but so does the return. It is return on return, and as the years go by, it is return on return on return, and so forth. The more the return—and the more time elapsed—the more impressive the resulting figure becomes. One dollar invested at 5 percent earns 5 cents (becoming $1.05) in one year, but earns $1.65 (becoming $2.65) if left for twenty years.

The basic formula:

$$\text{Future Value} = \text{Today's Value} \times (1 + \text{Rate of Return})^{\text{Number of Years}}$$

The following table tells how much $1 will be worth when left to compound for different numbers of years and at different percentages of return. You can see, for example, that $1 earning 5 percent per year (as mentioned previously) results in $2.65 in twenty years and then $7.04 after forty years.

The table also shows how greatly a different rate of return can affect the end result. Increasing the 5 percent return up to 8 percent causes the forty-year outcome to triple, going from $7.04 all the way to $21.72. (You may also notice the astounding $7,523.16 that a yearly return of 25 percent produces in forty years.)

It should be obvious how important it is to leave assets in place to take advantage of this power. That means don't touch the Golden Goose and, if at all possible, don't touch the eggs, either. Not only should you leave the assets alone, but it is also important to manage the return. A shortfall of even 1 percent or 2 percent can make a big difference over the long run. As a result, return reducers such as mutual fund management fees should be taken seriously.

Time Value of Money: Calculating Future Value

Interest Rate %	Number of Years							
	1	2	5	10	15	20	30	40
4.0%	$ 1.04	$ 1.08	$ 1.22	$ 1.48	$ 1.80	$ 2.19	$ 3.24	$ 4.80
5.0%	1.05	1.10	1.28	1.63	2.08	2.65	4.32	7.04
6.0%	1.06	1.12	1.34	1.79	2.40	3.21	5.74	10.29
7.0%	1.07	1.14	1.40	1.97	2.76	2.19	3.24	4.80
8.0%	1.08	1.17	1.47	2.16	3.17	4.66	10.06	21.72
9.0%	1.09	1.19	1.54	2.37	3.64	5.60	13.27	31.41
10.0%	1.10	1.21	1.61	2.59	4.18	6.73	17.45	45.26
12.0%	1.12	1.25	1.76	3.11	5.47	9.65	29.96	93.05
15.0%	1.15	1.32	2.01	4.05	8.14	16.37	66.21	267.86
20.0%	1.20	1.44	2.49	6.19	15.41	38.34	237.38	1,469.77
25.0%	1.25	1.56	3.05	9.31	28.42	86.74	807.79	7,523.16

Question 9: **How do my personal finance needs change with age?**

Personal finance is all about planning for life stages, that is, the major occurrences and phases in your life. While long-term goals may stay constant, intermediate goals and their priority will change. When young and starting out, the major objectives usually are buying a house, establishing assets and emergency reserves, and getting the compounding train rolling for retirement. Along the way, getting married and having children brings another set of financial needs—income and asset protection (insurance), college education, and so forth. Eventually, your needs will shift to health care, long-term care, and retirement.

Question 10: **How does inflation affect my personal finances?**

Inflation is one of those nagging uncertainties we can't do anything about, but it bears watching closely. At its roots, inflation may not have any real effect if your income rises with expenses and you maintain your savings plans. Asset returns also wouldn't be affected, for interest rates, investment price appreciation (driven by steadily inflating corporate earnings), and home appreciation would keep up. But unfortunately, inflation, particularly when out of control, doesn't affect everything equally. Expensive supply inputs may not be passed on by all corporations. Stagnant economic conditions resulting from price spikes in key economic inputs like oil may cause incomes to not keep up with inflation. Jobs may go away altogether. If you have fixed sums invested in long-term fixed income securities such as CDs, long-term Treasury bonds, etc., inflation will erode the buying power of these assets. So the prudent course is to track inflation and particularly the distortions it causes in the economy and to avoid owning too many vulnerable assets.

Chapter 2

BUDGETING AND MANAGING DAILY EXPENSES

Too much month left at the end of your money? Your first responsibility, as the one in charge of your finances, is to gain control of daily expenses. Without such control, you are far less likely to accumulate the necessary wealth to achieve financial objectives and improve your standard of living. Gaining control usually means some form of budgeting. While budgeting has a tedious and ominous sound to most, it doesn't really have to be so hard. It doesn't have to involve too much detail, and it can be revealing and even fun. Read on to find out how.

Question 11: **I just can't figure out where the money goes. Where should I look first?**

When it seems like every month should work out but it doesn't, it's time to do some *financial forensics*. Financial forensics is the first step to coming to grips with your finances and building a plan. Really, it's a detailed investigation of where everything goes, when and why.

Everybody's situation is different, but excess spending usually comes from (1) uncontrolled or impulse spending and (2) a failure to realize how much things cost. Impulse spenders buy first and consider consequences later—if at all—and usually end up buying more than intended. Need a pair of shoes? Resist the temptation to add a new shirt and a pair of slacks on impulse, no matter how cheap or attractive. Buying groceries? Resist the temptation to buy unneeded desserts, magazines, and snack foods. Think "can I afford it, and do I really need it, anyway?" Reward yourself for *not* buying.

Many people fail to realize how much things cost. A weekend getaway is nice, but despite today's low airfares, two tickets, a car rental, weekend hotel, meals, and a souvenir T-shirt are going to run $800 or more. An $800 weekend every month or two will strain most budgets and deny precious long-term savings. Even a day trip to a big city or an evening at a baseball game can run $100, $200, or more without blinking an eye. Know the costs—*all* costs—of what you do before you start.

Question 12: **What is budgeting, and how should I/we approach it?**

Budgeting is laying out a plan for income, expenses, and the difference between the two. It starts with financial forensics and continues by laying out a savings and spending plan. The savings plan usually has two components: (1) *off-the-top* savings come out of income before it has a chance to be spent (such as for 401(k) plan contributions, emergency funds, and other savings pools) and (2) *surplus* savings put aside amounts of income left after expenses. Budgeting is mapping the expenses, getting the commitment, executing the plan through the month, reviewing results, and informing and rewarding the participants.

Question 13: **What are the main components of a family budget?**

As long as it accomplishes the task, you can set up your budget any way you want. Adapted from this author's *Pocket Idiot's Guide to Living on a Budget, 2nd Edition* (Pearson, 2005), here are the major parts of a budget:

> *Gross Income* is employer-paid wages or salary plus any regular or irregular income from any source. Tracking and projecting gross income must be done with special care if you are self-employed.

> *Net Income* is Gross Income less tax withholdings, FICA, and for many, health insurance premiums and other uncontrollable expenses.

> *Off-the-top Savings* are removed from income before becoming available for spending, like retirement plan contributions. The definition can be expanded to include certain charitable contributions (like church tithing) and contingency "rainy day" funds to be set aside.

> *Obligations* are major and regular expenses tied to your chosen lifestyle. Many of these are contractual, such as home mortgages, rent, car loans, property tax, and day care/school tuition. Obligations must be paid before considering other expenses. Note that many are billed irregularly, such as property tax, and require funds to be set aside each month. This is one of the biggest budgeting challenges.

> *Necessities* are important must expenses tied to your lifestyle, but these can be adjusted through management. Groceries, utilities, telecommunications, school lunches, and home maintenance are examples. If you have a tight month, you can buy fewer or cheaper groceries, use less electricity, or put off that home repair project.

> *Discretionary Expenses* can be significantly modified or in some cases eliminated altogether. There are three subcategories of discretionary expenses:

- *Pocket Money* is a set amount of "ATM" money each family member gets for routine expenses not worth tracking individually. Pocket money makes small purchases such as lunches, snacks, Starbucks, etc. The amount should stay constant from week to week or month to month.
- *Family Allowance,* or "FAL", is a discretionary amount set aside for family activities such as entertainment, eating out, and similar expenses. The FAL can change depending on a month's circumstances.
- *Personal Allowance,* or "PAL", rounds out the expense categories and is an amount for every family member to spend as they please without further tracking. It covers clothing, entertainment, books, hobbies, and other discretionary expenses, and it can change considerably.

Surplus Savings, the final component of the family budget, occur in the happy circumstance that there is some money left over after expenses.

Question 14: **Do I/we need to track all expenses?**

Simply, all expenses must be counted, but not tracked separately. Catchall categories (see Question 13) such as Pocket Money, Family Allowance, and Personal Allowance make it unnecessary to write down every donut or cup of coffee. Doing it this way makes the budgeting process much easier.

Question 15: **What are the twelve steps of the budgeting process?**

Again, *The Pocket Idiot's Guide to Living on a Budget, 2nd Edition* (Pearson, 2005) gives a framework:

- *Understand income.* Know where income comes from, when and how regularly.
- *Understand expenses.* Financial forensics figures out where it goes, when, and how much.

■ *Set goals.* Financial planning determines long-term goals, but there will be short-term budget goals too—a family vacation, $300/month discretionary expenses for each family member to spend, or a new boat.

■ *Understand habits.* As an outcome of financial forensics, understand how you and the family handle money and communicate.

■ *Get savings and spending mechanisms in place.* Establish savings accounts, retirement plans, direct deposit, and special credit cards to manage individual and family allowances.

■ *Plan income.* Build a detailed plan for the next month and, if appropriate, the next twelve months.

■ *Plan obligations.* Build a schedule of major regular and irregular unavoidable expenses.

■ *Plan necessities.* Estimate variable but necessary items like food and utilities. Be careful to make expenses reflect the time of year—as in higher utility costs in midsummer and midwinter.

■ *Set aside pocket money.* Does each family member need $40, $60, or $100 to manage the little stuff through the week? Decide on a number and allow ATM withdrawals to that amount.

■ *Plan family allowance.* Set aside a certain amount for family entertainment, home improvement projects, and so forth. For some families, it is a good idea to have a separate credit card for these to better track expenses.

■ *Plan personal allowance.* Establish an amount each family member can spend, no questions asked. Again, a dedicated credit card might help.

■ *Balance and rebalance.* This is the all-important twelfth step. If there is enough income to meet requirements, perhaps with some left over, you're doing great! But for most families, there isn't enough to get by, so this step adjusts budgeted expenses and allowances to arrive at a viable plan.

Question 16: **Budgeting takes discipline and commitment from all family members. How do we get such commitment?**

Without commitment, budgeting doesn't work. The success formula will vary by family, but two common methods are to involve everybody in the budget-setting process and to reward performance. People involved in creating something tend to support it, so budgets shouldn't be handed down from above. Rewards for good performance—a generous holiday gift budget, a special vacation, or an end-of-year gift card from a favorite restaurant or retailer—always help. Keeping everybody informed of progress toward goals helps, too.

Question 17: **Must a budget be written down?**

The short answer: no. People stress out over the time and effort required to write down so many numbers. Some don't want to be reminded of difficult choices and tradeoffs. When starting out, it's important to write everything down to get familiar with the numbers and the outcome. But with experience the need to write it all down may go away. Budgets for family allowance and personal allowance will become second nature: you might have $300 to spend each month for your PAL. Detailed monthly budget calculation and recording becomes more important if income or expenses change a lot.

Question 18: **Why do budgets fail, and how can failure be avoided?**

Most budgets, like most of personal finance, fail if there is a lack of awareness, commitment, and control among all members of the family. A budget that is not followed or is stretched with a barrage of month-end excuses will fail. Once it fails a time or two, it's hard to get everyone restarted. Likewise, a budget that is fiction in the first place because income and expenses aren't well understood will also fail. So, like many things in life, diligence, attentiveness, honesty, and rewarded success will make it all right.

Chapter 3

HOW TO SAVE MONEY

S avings are a much talked about but much neglected part of individual finances. Indeed, personal savings—particularly ordinary, nonretirement, after-tax savings—have fallen to an all-time low, a fact that concerns many economists. Why are savings so elusive, especially in today's reduced income tax environment? Why are savings so neglected, when people know that so many important things such as a college education are more than ever their responsibility? Do people really not care about financial security? Do people really feel they will always be able to borrow their way out of problems? This chapter will give you some good ways to think about—and build—savings.

Question 19: Are savings really a single item in the financial plan, or are there different types of savings to consider?

A good financial plan segments savings into different categories for different purposes—an emergency fund, long-term savings, and short-term savings.

The "emergency" or "rainy day" fund is the first and most important savings category; it is set aside for income- and/or expense-related emergencies like job loss, unexpected car repair, medical expenses, etc. Most advisors consider about six months worth of income adequate. These savings should be used only for true emergencies and should be kept in liquid form, that is, immediately accessible with no penalty or cost.

Next on the list are long-term savings such as savings for retirement and college. Such savings, as implied, are socked away for the long term and are not to be touched but for the most dire circumstances. Regular contributions are good to keep building the "nest egg." As these savings are long-term in nature and scope, they should be invested to produce some return and to take advantage of compounding.

Finally—and lowest in priority—are short-term savings for such aspirational goals as vacations or major purchases like cars, boats, and so forth. Money should be set aside in other categories first, and ideally even the money needed for emergencies would come from this category before touching precious emergency fund savings. Different investment vehicles are used depending on the time horizon—short-term certificates of deposit (CDs) and credit union accounts often work well.

Question 20: **What are the best ways to save money?**

Saving money requires financial awareness and especially commitment and control. The best way to make savings happen is to have it pulled off the top of your paycheck before being available for other purposes. Directly depositing an amount into one or more savings accounts works well. Likewise, retirement plan contributions (401[k], IRA, or similar plans) should be regular and automatic, and they will accrue income tax savings for each month they are taken out. As such savings never enter the household checkbook; they don't get repurposed for other things. After a while, they aren't even missed. If you can't pull savings off the top, your standard of living is probably too high for your income.

Building home equity is another powerful way to achieve long-term savings. Aggressive mortgage payments, handled either as extra payments or through regular forced contributions using a shorter fifteen- or ten-year mortgage, work well. The savings buildup accelerates over time as interest expense takes a gradually smaller part of your payment. Sooner or later, you own your home, and you will have a nice chunk of savings. People should at least plan pay off their primary residence prior to retirement, and paying it off sooner makes it easier to reach other goals.

Question 21: **How much money do I/we need to save?**

This is a simple question with a complex answer. The first part is to figure out what you need, either a single amount or a "lump sum" capable of providing a "stream of income" (like a pension) over time.

Let's go for the more complex stream of income answer. Suppose you determine that you need $2,000/month for a twenty-year period in retirement. Using the following table, you can calculate a *distribution annuity*. This is the amount needed to support a constant payment based on an assumed rate of return on savings (assumed here at 5 percent) retained through the period.

Distribution Annuity Table

Interest Rate %	Number of Years							
	1	2	5	10	15	20	30	40
4.0%	1.0	1.9	4.5	8.1	11.1	13.6	17.3	19.8
5.0%	1.0	1.9	4.3	7.7	10.4	12.5	15.4	17.2
6.0%	0.9	1.8	4.2	7.4	9.7	11.5	13.8	15.0
7.0%	0.9	1.8	4.1	7.0	9.1	10.6	12.4	13.3
8.0%	0.9	1.8	4.0	6.7	8.6	9.8	11.3	11.9
10.0%	0.9	1.7	3.8	6.1	7.6	8.5	9.4	9.8
12.0%	0.9	1.7	3.6	5.7	6.8	7.5	8.1	8.2
15.0%	0.9	1.6	3.4	5.0	5.8	6.3	6.6	6.6
20.0%	0.8	1.5	3.0	4.2	4.7	4.9	5.0	5.0

For twenty years at 6 percent, the factor is 11.5. Take the annual amount needed ($24,000) and multiply by 12.5, giving $300,000. That is the amount that you need to save over twenty years to obtain the $2,000/month regular payment. (Note that this amount doesn't include taxes—if the source of funds is a retirement account funded with tax-deferred income, you pay taxes on the withdrawals.)

Now, to achieve $300,000 in savings, what do you need to save each year to make it happen? Enter the *accumulation annuity,* which works backward to figure out what needs to be set aside to achieve a certain sum.

Accumulation Annuity Table

Interest Rate %	Number of Years							
	1	2	5	10	15	20	30	40
4.0%	1.0	2.0	5.4	12.0	20.0	29.8	56.1	95.0
5.0%	1.0	2.1	5.5	12.6	21.6	33.1	66.4	120.8
6.0%	1.0	2.1	5.6	13.2	23.3	36.8	79.1	154.8
7.0%	1.0	2.1	5.8	13.8	25.1	41.0	94.5	199.6
8.0%	1.0	2.1	5.9	14.5	27.2	45.8	113.3	259.1
10.0%	1.0	2.1	6.1	15.9	31.8	57.3	164.5	442.6
12.0%	1.0	2.1	6.4	17.5	37.3	72.1	241.3	767.1
15.0%	1.0	2.2	6.7	20.3	47.6	102.4	434.7	1,779.1
20.0%	1.0	2.2	7.4	26.0	72.0	186.7	1,181.9	7,343.9

Suppose you have twenty years to accumulate the $300,000 and expect to earn the same 5 percent on your savings between now and then. Divide this amount by the figure in the table for twenty years, 5 percent (33.1), giving $9,063 in savings needed per year, or $755 per month. This is the amount to save, starting today, to achieve the $2,000 monthly payout starting twenty years from now.

If you play with these tables, you'll quickly see how the power of compounding works and how more time and higher returns accomplish so much more. You can find more information on this topic in this author's *The Everything® Personal Finance Book* (Adams Media, 2003).

Question 22: What's a good rule of thumb for how much I/we should save each month?

In an environment of frighteningly low savings rates, hovering around 1 percent nationwide, this is an especially timely question. A good rule for most individuals and households, barring special circumstances, is to strive to save 10 percent of gross income. That is, if you earn a $4,000 per month salary, try to work your savings to $400 per month. If you can save 10 percent after your 401(k) or retirement plan contribution, it is so much better. If you can save 10 percent after your equity portion of a mortgage payment, that's better still. In this way, you build retirement savings and after-tax savings for other goals.

Question 23: Where should I put my savings?

This question really moves toward the topic of investing. The short answer: savings vehicles should be set up to match the savings objective. The key variables are *liquidity* and *return*. Liquidity refers to the ease of penalty-free access to the funds; *return* refers to what you earn on the money. Higher liquidity means lower returns and vice versa. Other factors include trust in the financial institution and convenience.

Emergency or rainy day funds are best kept in liquid savings forms such as bank or credit union accounts with easy transfer to the household checking account. Long-term savings should be invested in securities—stocks, bonds, mutual funds, etc.—and usually should be held in specially set-up retirement plans or in brokerage accounts. Short-term savings depend on the time horizon and may be a mix of liquid investments.

Question 24: **I want to become a millionaire. Is that a realistic goal? How do I pull it off?**

The short answer is "yes, you can do it." As Thomas Stanley and William Danko so clearly demonstrated in *The Millionaire Next Door* (Longstreet, 1996), income helps, but the real key is financial discipline and stability. Millionaires are likely to be people who worked hard—but who also stayed put, drove old cars, and in general, resisted the temptation to consume and especially the temptation to show off. With the power of compounding, people who choose to persistently live below their means, keep their standard of living in check, and prioritize savings can make it even on ordinary incomes.

Chapter 4

CHOOSING AND USING A BANK

Banks, credit unions, and similar institutions are a fundamental and necessary step toward achieving your financial objectives. They provide services vital to day-to-day money management and, increasingly, services helpful for long-term financial planning. Banks are big, scary, and, if not used wisely, can be expensive and frustrating to work with. The following questions offer a few things to look for—and avoid—in choosing and using a bank.

Question 25: Are all banks the same? Why or why not?

First of all, there are different types of banks. Full-service banks usually have "bank" in the name—Bank of America, First Interstate Bank, or Citibank. They may be large and national or small and local, but they offer a wide range of services for consumers and local businesses, including checking, savings, and a full assortment of loan and credit services. Many are getting more involved in financial planning, insurance, and investments as regulatory restrictions ease. Savings and loans (S&Ls) are traditionally more consumer focused and do a lot of mortgage business, but they are moving toward becoming more full-service financial institutions (Washington Mutual, for example). Finally, credit unions, which are non-profit and usually have select memberships, offer many full-service banking services at a lower cost.

Due to relaxed regulation and mergers and consolidations, there has been some convergence among the types of institutions just described. Banks, S&Ls, and credit unions look increasingly similar. However, the subtle differences in their services and the quality of service merit careful consideration.

Question 26: **Big bank or small bank? Which is better?**

Big banks have gotten bigger, and like most of corporate America, they are very focused on delivering short-term profits to their investors, often at the expense of customer service. Unless you bring an exceptional amount of business (i.e., money), you'll be just a number. In today's banking world that might not be all bad, however. Big banks have many branch offices across a wide range of states, and you can get banking services—and free ATM withdrawals—just about wherever you go. Bigger banks are more likely to offer "24/7" banking service and Internet-based banking—although don't be fooled, these offerings are not just for your benefit, as they lower the bank's costs, too. In today's world of (mostly) electronic banking through ATMs, phones, and the Internet, big banks just might be okay. But if you have complex banking issues—in particular, if you have small business banking needs—small local or regional banks might be better suited to your needs.

Question 27: **What kinds of banking services will I need?**

Today's households almost certainly need a checking account, and the convenience of a checking account "debit" card is becoming increasingly attractive. Likewise, free and accessible ATM services are essential for cash access. Some form of savings vehicle to accumulate off-the-top savings (see Chapter 3) from deposited income is important, as is "direct deposit" to capture this income in the first place. Rounding out the essentials picture is some form of overdraft protection, in order to avoid high fees and exposure from accidentally overdrawing your checking account.

Other services run the gamut from loans and safety deposit boxes to full financial planning services, insurance, investments, college planning, and even automated banking and payment services. Some people like the "one-stop shop" approach to managing their finances, while others will do the legwork to go to different places: banks for day-to-day banking and specialists for financial planning services. It's a tradeoff based on the quality and convenience of services locally available, but be sure to properly assess this quality—and the cost—of these services before choosing. Banks, while offering everything, may not offer the best services or the best deal, and they often use insurance and loan services to subsidize traditional day-to-day banking operations.

Question 28: **Which bank should I choose and why?**

The "fast, friendly, and effective" model for choosing most products and services certainly applies to choosing a bank. First, for the "effective" part, you should look for a bank offering the right balance of services at the right price. Look closely at checking account fees (and the required balances needed to avoid them) and fees for services such as overdraft protection, "roaming" ATM use, excessive transactions, and balance inquiries. Examine rates of return offered on savings and, in some cases, checking accounts, although this usually isn't a major deciding factor—you're looking for money management, not investing return.

Next is the "fast" part. Does the institution have convenient locations with convenient hours? Convenient hours have become less important as more people bank with ATMs, by telephone, and on the Internet. (Checking the quality and cost of the latter two methods is worthwhile.)

Finally, the "friendly" part is still important. Does the bank treat you like a customer? Do bank officers and telephone customer service agents treat you with respect? Are they flexible? This is hard to know in advance, but typically the smaller the institution, the better. Of course, local word-of-mouth assessments are important.

Question 29: How many checking accounts should we have?

Household budgets tend to function more smoothly if there is a single household checking account into which all income is deposited and out of which all bills and monthly expenses are paid. It is simply easier to keep track, and since most checking accounts cost money for checks and processing fees, it is cheaper. Personal spending by individual family members is usually better managed using cash pocket money and a personal credit card. There are exceptions: separate checking accounts make sense for children away at college, for example. For those in their late teens and adults with their own earned income, separate checking accounts are a good financial learning exercise and probably make family expense control easier.

Question 30: What are the biggest banking mistakes to avoid?

Used carefully and properly, bank services are clean and relatively free of cost. Banks make some money lending your deposits to others at higher rates. But for small depositors and people who mainly use checking services, banks really make their money on fees. Fees start with monthly checking fees and check printing and escalate rapidly into overdraft charges, overdraft protection fees, stop-payment services, and so forth. The $2 your bank charges for a foreign bank ATM withdrawal plus the $1.50 the originating bank charges is a hefty bite out of the $20 you put into your pocket. Moral: avoid such specialized "safety net" services. Manage your finances to avoid overdrafts and plan ATM withdrawals in advance. Don't feel obliged to use a bank's major credit card (VISA, MasterCard). Typically such cards are more expensive and burdened with higher fees. Likewise, their loans and other services may not be the best deal.

Question 31: **I've heard a lot about online banking. What is it, and is it right for me?**

Online banking is still in its early adoption phase. Customers particularly adapted to doing things online are using it, but it hasn't hit the mainstream. It has the compelling capability to put everything in front of you, allowing minor transactions with a click of a mouse—including paying bills—saving time and making it easier to track your finances. But today it is still burdened with excessive fees, especially given that the bank saves money on its operations (by avoiding manual check processing, for instance). Not every bill can be paid online. Finally, time spent logging on can be a nuisance, especially compared to a simple trip to the checkbook. Nevertheless, online banking probably is the future. One would expect to pay more someday for traditional banking services with online banking, ATM debit cards, cell phone wireless banking, etc., to replace them.

Chapter 5

ABOUT DEBT AND CREDIT

For better or for worse, debt is the high-octane fuel powering today's economy and the finances of most individuals. The advent of consumer credit and the debt resulting from its use is a relatively modern phenomenon emerging in the early twentieth century. The coming of universal national credit cards and networks like Visa and MasterCard made the use of credit more popular and far more convenient than paying with cash. Today most retail transactions use some from of plastic, and most other major purchases, such as cars or homes, are made with some form of debt. Like any high-octane fuel, credit and debt can get you into trouble if used improperly. Read on to learn how to use this powerful tool without getting burned.

Question 32: What is the difference between debt and credit, and why is it so important?

People get these two terms confused all the time. *Debt* is an amount you already owe someone, to be paid off with interest within a specific time period. Debt represents money already spent, to be paid back with dollars earned in the future. *Credit,* on the other hand, represents the *potential* to borrow money to buy something. Credit reflects financial strength and discipline—the *ability* to pay. Thus, credit is a good thing, and debt—most debt, anyway—is a bad thing. Many people get this confused. You should work to reduce debt and improve credit. Note: this doesn't mean acquiring more credit cards, but instead improving your credit score. For an explanation of what that entails, read on.

Question 33: **My rich aunt tells me all debt is bad, but I'm still not sure. Is there such a thing as good debt?**

It's probably okay to assume that all debt is "bad" and that the less debt you have the better your financial footing. With that said, some debt used for some things can be "good," that is, beneficial to your long-term finances. For example, a mortgage used to acquire a home (1) provides a place to live and (2) allows ownership of a solid asset historically likely to grow in value. An educational loan can boost your career. Even short-term "opportunistic" debt used to buy something you need at a bargain price can be "good" debt, like using a credit card to buy future holiday gifts during an August sale. Some debt is just plain necessary—to replace a broken car, fix a roof, etc. Now comes the "bad debt"—debt incurred to support excessive spending beyond your standard of living or debt that exceeds your ability to pay it off quickly.

Question 34: **How do people fall into the debt trap? How does one avoid it?**

There are lots of possible reasons for becoming overextended with debt. Most boil down to poor spending habits, unforeseen expenses, or poor credit management.

Poor spending habits include impulse buying, living beyond one's means, and striving to "keep up with the Joneses." *Unforeseen expenses* can be broken down into truly unpredictable expenses—car repairs or replacing the lawnmower—or those that are predictable but nobody predicted them, such as that semiannual insurance bill that somehow didn't make it into the spending plan. In either instance, failure to plan and lack of emergency or "rainy day" funds will land these expenses solidly into the debt column. Finally, *poor credit management* habits—minimal payments and too many credit cards—will deepen the debt cycle already underway.

The bottom line: living beyond one's means and having a lack of awareness, commitment, and control will roll the debt snowball downhill at an alarming pace.

Question 35: **What different types of credit are available?**

Most consumers know about credit cards, but it helps to recognize other forms of consumer debt and how to use them properly.

Revolving credit allows borrowing up to a predetermined limit for an undefined period of time with a minimum but otherwise undefined payment. Old debt is replaced by new debt through new charges or purchases each period, thus the term "revolving." Once commonly offered by individual merchants, credit cards are now the primary example.

Installment loans are made for a fixed amount and have a fixed payment over a fixed time usually at a fixed interest rate. They usually come from special finance companies for large purchases; car loans are a good example.

Mortgage loans are long-term loans for the specific purpose of buying real estate, which in turn secures the loan. Since failure to pay results in foreclosure, transferring the asset to the lender, the lender can afford to offer lower interest rates.

Equity lines combine the best features of mortgage loans and revolving credit. The asset secures the loan, giving interest rates far lower than unsecured revolving credit. Time periods are defined but usually are long term (five to ten years), and payments are indefinite. Interest is usually income tax deductible. The danger: these loans are so attractive and easy to use that they tempt people into borrowing and putting their house on the line for bad debt.

Question 36: **What is a credit score and how do I get one? Why is it important?**

A *credit score* is a single number used in the lending industry essentially to measure your reliability and ability to pay debts. A complex model developed by Fair, Isaac & Co ("FICO Score") assesses your creditworthiness from your payment history, amount of income, current and potential debt, and employment.

Scores are furnished on a 300–850 scale where 850 represents near-perfect credit and 300 is totally uncreditworthy. Scores below 500, representing the lowest 1 percent of the population, are projected to have an 87 percent default rate. Forty-nine percent fall between 700–799, with a 2 to 5 percent projected delinquency rate. Your own score is available for $12.95 at *www.myfico.com*.

Credit scores are obviously important for lenders to determine if, how much, and at what rate to lend you money. People with low scores will pay higher interest rates, get smaller loans, or will be denied credit altogether. Interestingly and controversially, credit scores are sometimes used as a general character assessment for insurance and employment qualification. The bottom line: keeping this score high by managing credit well is a good idea.

Question 37: **How can I improve my credit rating?**

Maintaining reasonable amounts of debt and paying bills on time are the main ways to keep your score high. Late or nonpayments hurt more than anything else. Beyond that, evidence of stability through employment, home ownership, or long-term renting all help.

If you have a poor score, the first step is to get a credit report through MyFICO (*www.myfico.com*) or from any of the three major credit agencies (Experian, Equifax, or TransUnion). The report doesn't just show the score; it shows all known loans and credit cards, payment history, and missed payments. Mistakes can unnecessarily harm your score; such mistakes should be taken up with the lender. Start good debt habits immediately by paying on time or early.

Beyond payments, other factors such as excessive balances, balances at or near credit limits, and too much shifting between accounts will hurt your rating. Car, student, and other types of loans all count. Too much credit, even if not used, will hurt your score. Lenders are skeptical if you have drawers full of Visa, AMEX, and other credit cards; the potential is there to get into trouble. Cancel the credit cards you don't need. The bottom line: use credit modestly and wisely.

Question 38: **If I switch to another credit card, will that adversely affect my credit rating?**

The answer depends on your credit profile and why you're switching. If you have a long credit history, pay off balances regularly, and seldom apply for credit, it is pretty much a nonevent. However, if you move balances frequently or have recently applied for credit elsewhere, it will likely affect your credit score, albeit temporarily. If you're switching accounts to try to stretch out payments or lower the interest rate on an excessive balance, the credit-scoring agencies will notice. But most people find the need to change credit cards every now and then—due to a move, a more attractive offer, better customer service, etc. If your credit history is otherwise acceptable, the consequences should be minimal.

Question 39: **What is the difference between debit and credit cards?**

While they look similar, they are very different. A *debit card* is really a means to pay electronically with whatever funds you have in the linked account. A debit card transfers funds immediately and electronically from your account to the payee's. With a *credit card*, a financial intermediary (usually a bank) pays the payee immediately, while you pay the bank back at a later date. Debit card spending is limited to your on-hand balance, while credit card spending is limited only by your credit limit.

The debit card may say "Visa" or "MasterCard" on it, but that only broadens acceptance and allows access to payment systems, not the credit provisions of the card supplier.

Debit cards are gradually overtaking checks and cash because they are simpler and almost universally accepted. They will not work for renting cars, for there is no other binding promise to pay for excess use, damage, etc., as is implied by the credit limit on a credit card. The downside of debit cards: it is harder to track expenses. There is no equivalent to a check register (except monthly statements or online summaries), and it is almost too easy to whip out the debit card and forget about it.

Question 40: **What different kinds of credit cards are there?**

There are many ways to classify credit cards. For this answer, it makes sense to describe major credit cards, "charge" cards, and specialty cards.

Major credit cards include the common Visa, MasterCard, and Discover, usually issued by or through major banks. There are several special types:

> *Gold and Platinum credit cards* have some preferential services (like product warranty and other kinds of protective services) and convey some degree of status but usually cost more (higher fees, interest).

> *Reward credit cards* return some form of incentive for use— airline mileage or even a portion of your purchases in cash. Mileage cards are ubiquitous and usually cost a little more, but frequent users like business travelers can accumulate a large sum of miles essentially free. The Discover card is the prime example of the cash reward card, refunding up to 1 percent of purchases. While interest rates are high, there are no other costs, and it is really a hidden gem among cards especially if you pay off balances monthly.

> *Affiliate credit cards,* like GM MasterCard or L.L.Bean Visa, offer product discounts and certain other benefits from the affiliated supplier. Some are connected to charitable causes.

Charge cards look and work like credit cards but require balances to be paid off monthly; that is, there is no credit extended. American Express is the prime example, offering many specialized services albeit at a fairly high cost.

Specialty credit cards are issued by single businesses such as department stores and oil companies. These cards can be handy for special budget items or to take advantage of special sales, but most of these companies accept the major credit cards, too. So given that it is easier to keep track of credit use with fewer cards and that your credit score will likely improve, it is best to minimize use of these cards.

Question 41: Reward cards sound like a good idea, but what are the pitfalls?

Reward cards allow you to build up mileage points, discounts, or even cash. But the downside usually is higher credit costs. Most reward cards have relatively high interest rates and annual membership fees. The ever-popular Chase United Mileage Plus Visa carries a 14.99 percent interest rate (in late 2004) for good customers and a $60 annual fee; from other card offers, it is possible to get 10 percent interest rates and no annual fees. So is it worth it? If you spend $500 a month on the credit card, you'll get 6,000 flyer miles per year—roughly one-quarter of an airline round-trip (at 25,000 miles for a U.S. round-trip coach ticket). If you value that ticket above $240, one-quarter of it pays for the $60 annual fee, assuming you pay off your balance. But if you only spend $200 a month or never travel, it probably isn't worth it. Discover still offers the notable exception: 14.54 percent interest rates and no annual fee and a 1 percent cash reward, which is money that can be used anywhere. The bottom line: choose your rewards carefully, do some math to make sure they "pencil out," and pay off your balance each month.

Question 42: **What credit cards should I carry?**

To a degree, the answer is a matter of personal preference; "whatever works best" is really the right answer. One good approach is to allow each family member (over eighteen) a major credit card for their personal allowance (see Chapter 2). This can be a normal, a reward, or an affiliate credit card; it really doesn't matter. Family expenses can be kept on yet another joint credit card. Discover works well for this, for the 1 percent rebates can take some of the bite out of expensive home improvements, family travel, and so forth. Finally, you may want to have a handful—though not too many—of specialty credit cards. For most families, it is hard to keep track of more than two or three balances, so the need for any credit cards beyond that number needs to be carefully justified.

Question 43: **How do I choose a credit card?**

Choosing a credit card is similar to anything else; examine the costs, features, and benefits and then decide. Key credit card costs include annual fees, interest rates (relevant only if you don't plan to pay off balances monthly), and late payment fees. There are other fees for exceeding credit limits, but hopefully these will be irrelevant for you. Features and benefits include the obvious rewards and affiliate benefits. But there are also more subtle items: length of *grace period* (the period between statement close and payment due) and even the geographic location of the credit card issuer. Payments mailed to Delaware from the West Coast take a while with erratic delivery, creating opportunities for late payments and fees. The *basis* used to calculate interest is important. Is it the average daily balance or something else? Customer service is also a factor. Are the agents accommodating and willing to give you slack if you're late once in a while? There is no way to tell for sure from the credit card offer; word of mouth is a good resource. Don't be fooled into thinking that an affiliate credit card tied to a company with excellent service means you get great service on the credit card; these cards are usually run by big banks with few real ties to the affiliate.

Question 44: **What is my financial responsibility if I lose a credit card?**

By law, your financial liability is limited to:

- *Nothing* after you report the lost credit card to the issuing company
- *$50* for any fraudulent charges incurred before the loss is reported (and many issuers will waive even this amount)
- *Nothing* if you still have the card but the number was used fraudulently, that is, in a mail or Internet transaction

These protections are reassuring. In addition, credit card issuers employ highly sophisticated audit models to ferret out potentially bogus charges. If you live in Arizona and typically charge $200 a month for small purchases, a $5,000 money order purchased in Iowa will merit a verifying phone call from the issuer. You're well served to take that call and resolve the matter quickly but don't offer too much information to the caller, such as your complete Social Security number. There have been scams around this type of call. While there is some protection, it's in your best interest to carry a minimal number of credit cards and keep track of charges yourself. Don't buy credit card loss protection insurance, as you probably don't need it.

Question 45: **Why is identity theft so important, and how do I guard against it?**

Identify theft has always been a problem, but it has escalated substantially in recent years as electronic commerce has grown more pervasive and far-flung. It has become easier to obtain a person's identify, more lucrative to use it fraudulently, and harder to catch the culprits. With a bogus identity, anyone anywhere in the world can set up a charge account, purchasing anything from anywhere with little real chance of getting caught. Once your complete identity gets out there, it can be bought and sold further.

Identity theft goes beyond stealing the carbons of your credit card from the trash. While a certain amount of fraud can be perpetrated with this information, it is really your complete identity and especially your Social Security number that should be guarded at all costs. A complete ten-digit Social Security number, address, birth date, and a little family history will allow criminals to clone you at will. The upshot: you shouldn't carry your SSN on your person, nor should you give it out to anyone *contacting you,* by phone or on the Internet. Only give it out when absolutely needed and when you initiate the contact. Watch your incoming and outgoing mail, and mail sensitive documents, like tax returns, at post offices or in public mailboxes if you have reason to be suspicious. If your state uses your SSN as a driver's license number, ask for a different number.

The Federal Trade Commission offers a handy Web site discussing the nature, prevention, and resolution of identity theft at *www.consumer.gov/idtheft.* It's worth your time to take a trip through the Web site to become familiar with this topic.

Question 46: **My wallet/purse was stolen. What happens now?**

The first step is to list to the extent possible what was contained in the item: which credit cards, forms of identification, and financial documents. Consider all forms of such documents—passports, personal checks, pay stubs, and bank statements, for instance. Contact credit card companies immediately. This not only avoids the $50 liability explained in Question 44, but also alerts companies to your situation and begins the process of getting this information back to credit bureaus and agencies. Next, if personal checks or bank statements are involved, notify your bank. You will need a new checking account and account number. It's also a good idea to notify the major credit bureaus—Equifax, Experian, and TransUnion—directly (see the Federal Trade Commission Web site mentioned in Question 45 to find out how). Then you'll need to quickly report a passport loss to the Department of State and renew your driver's license with the state motor vehicle bureau.

While losing a wallet or a purse is a nuisance, most institutions are set up to handle this sort of situation and generally do it with relative ease and expedience. The bank portion is the most difficult and stressful hurdle, particularly if you have outstanding but unpaid checks, which the bank may seem to want to do little about. But you should be up and running financially within one week or so, while bearing little in the way of financial cost. If the situation is urgent—for example, if you are traveling—credit card issuers and local law enforcement agencies will help you get what you need in the form of identification and credit to complete your travel.

Again, the Federal Trade Commission identity theft Web site at *www.consumer.gov/idtheft* is an excellent resource.

Question 47: **Should I pay off credit cards each month?**

In a word, yes. Monthly payment in full is a sign that your finances are healthy and that your consumption is matched to your income. It also saves interest and preserves credit to borrow when you really need something. Sharp personal financiers use time payments only if they save a lot on the purchase, as with a postseason clothing sale or similar purchase.

Question 48: **What are the real and hidden costs of credit?**

First of all, *credit cost* is really *debt cost*, an additional cost of spending more than you have. The obvious costs are the interest paid to fund the debt, which can often be 21 percent per year. Annual fees and charges can be $80 per card for the fancier major cards. Those are the obvious costs; less obvious costs are late payment charges (averaging about $30 and going up to $40), interest rate increases triggered by any late payment on your credit record, and cash advance fees ($5 up to 2 percent of the balance advanced, plus interest from the day of withdrawal). Even less obvious is the higher interest rate on other future loans if you have overextended credit. The best credit habits (no-fee cards, on-time in-full payment each month, no cash advances) keep the cost of credit relatively low and maybe at zero. But poor habits can cost hundreds of dollars each year per card.

Question 49: **What is "APR"?**

APR stands for Annualized Percentage Rate. You'll see loans quoted at a 7.5 percent nominal rate and an APR of 7.79 percent. What does that mean? It means there are additional loan charges—a credit report, an annual fee—that must, by law, be calculated into the APR. APR allows clear "apples-to-apples" comparison between loans.

Question 50: **In general, how should I use credit cards?**

Prudent individuals use credit cards primarily as a convenient means of payment, that is, as an alternative to cash or checks. It is simply easier, and month-end summaries make it easier to track expenses. When used strictly as a means of payment, bills are paid in full each month. But there are situations where extended credit can make sense to capture a special low price on something needed anyway. Saving 20 percent or more usually justifies the interest expense, if it is planned carefully and paid off quickly. Credit cards are usually the tool to handle emergencies, such as an unexpected car repair. Use of credit cards to fund bad debt or to accumulate airline miles is the wrong way.

Question 51: **How do most people get into trouble with credit cards?**

The root cause of credit card trouble is spending too much. But poor habits and management of credit balances can make the problem much worse.

Making minimum payments or too small a payment is usually the first error. A minimum payment of $20 on a $1,000 balance looks attractive, but it will take ten years to pay it off. The total interest paid over that time, at 21.5 percent, is $1,548. If you pay $50 each month, it only takes two years to pay it off, and the total interest cost would be $248.

Getting too many credit cards or chasing lower interest rates by transferring balances from card to card often ends up in trouble, too. The temptation to lower interest rates is good in a way, for it lowers credit expense and allows faster payoffs. But many people become too focused on the *rate*—not the *balance*—and somehow bad debt starts to become acceptable because the interest rate is only 9.9 percent. When transferring balances, it is hard to really stop using the old card, and soon multiple balances proliferate on multiple cards.

Consolidating credit card balances to another card or to a home equity line is another trap. Wiping the slate clean across the many credit cards seems attractive, but the usual reality is that balances creep back onto the clean cards. You must then service those balances and a large consolidated balance, too.

Question 52: **People tell me that a second mortgage or home equity line is a good way to carry debt or restructure the debt I have. Is this right, and what are the advantages and disadvantages?**

There are two inherent advantages of using home equity financing to pay off, or refinance, other debt. First, interest costs are lower, often by as much as 15 percent; second, interest is usually tax deductible. But the list of disadvantages is long. First and most obvious: you are putting your home on the line. This is a big deal. Second, those "clean" credit card balances are likely to reappear, negating the advantage. Third, interest rates are variable and fairly sensitive to the economic environment, and your interest costs may grow and, in any case, are unpredictable. Finally, you use up good credit that really should be applied to other long-term purposes, if at all—big purchases, emergency use, and so forth. So you're better off focusing on eliminating the debt or avoiding it altogether. Resist the temptation to use this attractive form of financing to mask poor debt habits.

Question 53: **I get hit several times a day, often by telemarketers, with proposals to cash out home equity through refinancing. When does this make sense?**

With 2004 interest rates at an all-time low and home appreciation at a near all-time high, it seems to make sense to cash out at least some portion of equity. But like most investment decisions, you must decide if there are other better investments. In this case, you are incurring an interest cost and taking on more risk of losing the property. So generally it makes sense if used to remodel the home (thus adding value) or for some other expense that will produce long-term returns (such as education to build a career). Using home equity to finance college education for children can be okay, but other forms of college financing should also be examined. Using home equity to finance retirement should be used as a last resort. Cashing out to invest in the stock market should be done only with great care. You must achieve a return greater than interest paid, plus some premium to compensate for the risk taken. There may be an exception if the home is your only asset and you are trying to diversify. Clearly, cashing out to support unnecessary short-term spending is a no-no.

Question 54: **I have a $30,000 balance on my Gold MasterCard. What should I do?**

First of all, you're not alone. While the average household credit card and installment debt runs about $9,000, many people find themselves in such a big hole. There are many ways to get there—job loss, frequent job-related moves, expenses for starting a business, or just plain negligent, out-of-control spending.

The first step is to stop spending now. Put the credit card in a drawer. Next, you should review the interest rate and look for a lower one if it makes sense. Paying 18 percent means $5,400/year in interest cost—a reduction even to 10 percent would save $2,400/year. While in most situations it's wiser to focus on the balance rather than on the interest rate, here the numbers are large enough—costly enough—to move to a lower rate if possible. That lower rate may be found with a home equity line if you have one available, but care must be taken not to jeopardize your home ownership and to avoid getting deeper into debt.

Once you determine where to carry the debt, you must carefully budget a payment schedule to pay it down. The plan should take the payment off the top, that is, before other spending. Spending will usually have to be cut. It can help to get a quick income boost somewhere else through a second or part-time job. When set aside, that income can service the debt and then provide a financial reward when finally paid off.

Along the way you should do a financial forensic investigation to determine why you got into the situation the first place. With the right combination of awareness, commitment, and control most people emerge okay and with a good financial lesson under their belts.

Chapter 6

MAKING BIG PURCHASES

*B*ig purchases are purchases of the sometimes inevitable, sometimes merely desirable things that make life go on—or go on with more pleasure. Cars are the quintessential big-ticket item. You need a car, and most people can't simply write a check to buy one. Other big purchases range from home appliances, furnaces, and other necessities to such pleasures as big-screen televisions, boats, and new patio furniture. Regardless of the purchase, careful planning is important. Without the kind of planning described below, these purchases become budget busters and dead weight in the way of paying monthly expenses and achieving other more important financial objectives.

Question 55: **In general, what's the best way to plan for big-ticket purchases?**

The best way is to build a savings component into your budget and set aside funds off the top of your income. These funds can be separated into a different account or remain a designated portion of your primary savings account. The need and timing of the purchase doesn't always allow saving in advance, so purchasing on credit is okay if carefully planned. Calculate the monthly payment and put it in the budget. Credit purchases are best used to take advantage of a big price break; the overall purchase cost will be lower even including the cost of the credit. But don't overuse this rationale; saving with sale prices is a bad idea if you end up over your head. Finally, you must look at the long-term *cost of ownership*, not just the purchase price. It is a common trap, for example, for boat buyers to overlook the cost of maintenance, storage, mooring, insurance, fuel, etc.

Question 56: **I think I need a new car. What alternatives should I think about?**

Buying a car is a frustrating and emotional experience that can really set back your finances. Yet, sooner or later, nearly all have to endure this pain. While challenging, the best advice is to keep cool and use as rational an approach as possible.

The first question: do you really need a new car? If you clean and/or fix the old one, will it do the job? A $1,500 repair is onerous but may be cheaper than depreciation on a new car. In many states, such an amount is less than the transaction costs—sales tax, registration fees, and difference in insurance premiums—involved in buying a new car. Do the math and you might be surprised. Finally, before doing anything, spend $25 on a good full-service car wash; you might be surprised at how much more you like your current car when it's really clean.

If it's still "yes, I really do need a new car," the shopping process begins. Research and selection process can't be fully addressed here, but you should at least examine alternatives to buying a brand new car. Auto retailers like CarMax and America's Car Mart bring well-qualified cars at attractive prices and without the usual vagaries of buying a used car.

Question 57: **I really do need a new car now. Lease it or buy it?**

Leasing is a means of financing a car through what amounts to an extended rental period. With a lease, you get possession and all normal vehicle operating costs for a specified period, usually twenty-four to forty-eight months. Payments appear attractive; they are less than a typical car loan payment because you don't build equity. At the end of the lease, you turn in the car, owning nothing, and ideally owing nothing.

There are two major drawbacks. First, as mentioned, you build no equity in the car and start from scratch at the beginning of each lease period. Second, most lease contracts have modest mileage allowances, often only 10,000 to 12,000 miles per year, beyond which substantial per mile charges apply. Damage to the car can be assessed and billed at high prices. Initial down payments are lost completely, and transaction costs (taxes, registration) occur each time you enter a new lease.

Leases can make sense in certain short-term situations: if your business requires a relatively new car every two to three years (e.g., a real estate agent) or if you anticipate changes in your automotive needs. Otherwise, most are better off with regular purchase financing. Most importantly, don't choose a car based on financing. Separate the purchase decision from the financing decision—otherwise you're likely to play into the dealer's hand.

Question 58: **I need a new refrigerator, and the appliance store is offering "six months same as cash." Should I be impressed?**

"Six months same as cash" means you don't have to make a payment for six months. It is essentially free financing for the period, which can be attractive, but be careful. When the free (or sometimes reduced) interest period expires, any remaining balance will be charged full interest retroactive through the entire ownership period. That is, if you buy a $1,500 refrigerator and have a $1,000 balance in six months, you will be charged $90 back interest (if the normal annual interest rate is 18 percent), and monthly interest will start at that rate until the balance is paid. Late payments on other debt may also trigger normal interest. So if you can pay it off in the "free" period, go for it, but if there's any chance you can't, look out.

Question 59: **My family really wants a new $3,000 plasma television. How should I evaluate whether I can afford it?**

The first step is to appraise where you are with your other finances. Are you keeping up with your plan, including paying routine expenses, covering possible emergencies, and achieving other savings goals? If the answer is "yes," you're ready to consider this purchase.

The next step is to evaluate the purchase itself. Is it really necessary to spend $3,000 on this luxury item? Are there less expensive alternatives? LCD TV? More traditional large-screen technologies? Where on the "technology curve" are we? Is this product likely to be outdated in a few years? Will the price come down? Research—not just one salesperson's opinion—is required. Read magazines, look at Web sites, and talk to "smart friends" who follow the technology.

Finally, when the choice is made, consider the financing alternatives. Decide if it makes sense to tap an already-existing savings pool (without compromising some other objective). If savings aren't available, does your budget carry the capacity to service a new debt? Can you get a discount by buying today instead of tomorrow? If the answer is "no," the time may not be right. Look into buy something cheaper or later and prepare for it.

Question 60: **What are the alternatives to buying expensive, new stuff?**

Big purchases, when handled poorly, can become the budget buster we all dread, setting finances back for a long time. Before buying anything—from a pressure washer to a new car—consider the following:

> *Clean it.* It is amazing how much more we like a car or an old gas grill with a little time and effort spent to really clean it up. The cleaning can be done professionally at a car wash or

with old-fashioned elbow grease. In either way, the amount of money you'll save over a lifetime with this approach can be well worth it.

Fix it. It may not make sense to fix a $25 toaster, but bigger items like cars and lawnmowers may cost you less in the long run to fix. A rule of thumb: any repair that costs less than 40 percent of replacement purchase price should be seriously considered. Also to consider: does replacement also achieve other cost savings, like reduced energy usage?

Rent it. Renting doesn't work for everything, but if something is used once in a while and is expensive to acquire and maintain, renting can work well. Think about renting large home maintenance tools such as pressure washers and rototillers. Consider renting recreational items used only occasionally, like boats and campers.

You may still decide to buy, but if you consider these alternatives, you'll at least feel better about your purchase.

Question 61: My friends always try to impress me with their purchases—boats, vacation homes, and so forth. Should I be impressed?

The general rule: so-called "luxury" or lifestyle expansion purchases should only be undertaken once other financial needs are met. If monthly expenses are met, emergency reserves set aside, college and retirement plans on track, and debt levels within control (and could be paid off immediately if necessary), you may consider such purchases. Boats, motor homes, vacation homes, swimming pools, timeshare units, and sports cars can break any budget—especially when costs of ownership are included. These purchases should be avoided by most. Plan carefully.

Question 62: **Should I buy the extended warranty?**

Extended warranties can give some peace of mind, especially when buying complex products like automobiles. However, be aware that many retailers and manufacturers make more money selling the warranty than the product. That should tell you something. Also, many credit cards, especially the premium gold or platinum variety, offer an extended warranty of their own on items purchased—for free. Finally, the cost of the warranty can run 40 to 50 percent of the product price; you're better off to save and replace—to self-insure—the unlikelihood of failure. The quality of most products sold today is high enough that failure rates are relatively low. There may be some products, like laptop computers, where the warranty extends to cover accidental damage; this can be helpful if you anticipate "rough" ownership, but be careful not to pay too much.

PART II

Planning for Lifetime Goals

Chapter 7

BUYING A HOME

Speaking of big purchases, let's address one of life's biggest financial decisions—buying a home. The size and importance of this purchase should not be underestimated, and the technicalities of financing should be well understood. A bad decision can lead to thousands of dollars of unnecessary expense later or even the loss of your home. Likewise, doing it right can bring enormous personal and financial rewards. Few events have greater impact on family life or finances. More than anywhere else, you need to separate the purchase decision from the financing decision and keep a cool, rational head throughout the process.

Question 63: Everybody says buying a home brings a number of financial benefits. Are they right? Why?

In most situations, the short answer is "yes." Buying a home to live in not only provides needed shelter and gives a source of pride, but it also helps financially. Here's how:

- *Forced saving.* With traditional mortgage financing, a defined and steadily growing portion of your payment regularly goes to equity—your ownership in the home.
- *Tax benefits.* Home ownership brings a large and unique tax break in the form of a $250,000 ($500,000 if married) capital gains exclusion on home appreciation. For most homeowners, this is the biggest tax break they'll see in life. Additionally, mortgage interest cost is income tax deductible for most people.
- *Safe appreciation.* Real estate price appreciation has been relatively steady over time compared to most assets, and homes provide a hedge against inflation.
- *Reduced need for other things.* Own a home, and you'll feel less compelled to take that $1,000 weekend trip.
- *Opportunity to build "sweat equity."* The possibility of home improvement provides a unique opportunity to build wealth through your own labor and talents.

It is the synergy of these benefits that really brings financial success. Stand-alone factors like the mortgage interest deduction help but by themselves may not justify the purchase. Be keenly aware that not all home purchases work out, and many create other financial burdens like home maintenance.

Question 64: **What kind of house should I buy?**

Obviously location and personal taste play a big role in selecting a home. Financially, it helps to buy a home that you will be happy with for a long time, as moving costs and the buy/sell transactions involved are expensive. You want a place that, career transfers aside, you want to live in for five years or more. So it helps to stretch a little to buy something better, something you and your family will consider a "home," not just a "house." Adding "sweat equity" through your own improvements also helps in the long term, so look for a home that isn't perfect and that will benefit from improvement.

Question 65: **How do I tell if a home is overpriced?**

Rapid home price appreciation during 2001–2005 has brought this question into the spotlight. There is no perfect guide, but you should be wary of buying any asset experiencing rapid recent appreciation. Anything appreciating more than 10 percent per year is obviously growing faster than the economy and inflation as a whole, and such growth is unsustainable in the long term.

Certainly you'll want to review comparable sales in your area, which can be done by your realtor or through various real estate portals, like Yahoo!Real Estate or the National Association of Realtors *(www.realtor.com)*. But the rental return-on-investment model is another rational approach. If rented, would the rent on the property provide a reasonable return to the owner? If you're looking at a $400,000 home that would rent, by comparative analysis, for $1,200/month, that would provide an investor $14,400/year on $400,000, a mere 3.6 percent return before expenses. Is that a good return? No—either the rent is too low (unlikely) or the price is too high.

Question 66: **How much house can I afford?**

Your answer depends on both income and assets. The general rule holds that a mortgage payment should be no more than 28 percent of your gross income, although this rule has flexed a bit in recent years. If your earnings (combined earnings, if appropriate) are $75,000/year, then 28 percent of that figure would be $21,000/year, or $1,750/month. At a 6 percent mortgage interest rate for thirty years, that payment works backward into a loan amount of $291,885. With a traditional 20 percent down payment, that gives a maximum affordable value of $364,856. *Adjustable mortgages* (ARMs) can afford more, but keep in mind that payments will increase, demanding increased income to stay out of trouble. This scenario requires a fairly clean debt slate (with a monthly servicing cost for all other debts of less than 10 percent of gross income) and does not include other costs of home ownership, such as property taxes, homeowner's insurance, and maintenance.

Question 67: **Can I buy or sell a home without a realtor?**

The short answer: yes. While convenient, realtors are not required by law, and they can add a substantial transaction cost (usually 6 percent of purchase price) to the transaction. To be sure, as a buyer you don't avoid this fee by having the seller pay—it is ultimately built into the sale price of the home. The technicalities of a real estate contract aren't much more complex than standard income tax forms and vary by state. Get a copy of the standard real estate purchase contract used in your state (a filled-out example would be best). This isn't to say you don't need professional help; you should develop a relationship with an attorney and/or an escrow officer. These folks can give advice, help with technicalities, and should be able to help with forms. Sellers may offer to pay an escrow officer a small fee or gratuity for help, as they are typically paid only to finalize and record transactions. Marketing—finding buyers—is the biggest hurdle for do-it-yourself sellers. A professional approach with well-crafted newspaper ads, open houses, etc., usually works if your house is priced properly. Discount realtors can also be attractive, but be clear on what you're getting for the reduced fees of 2 to 3 percent.

Realtors help buyers find houses, but Internet resources are improving. The once exclusive "Multiple Listing Service" is generally available online. You can enter your search criteria and select homes—even those for sale by owner—with a click of a mouse.

Question 68: **Obviously the mortgage is a big factor. What kind should I get and why?**

Choosing a mortgage is more complex than can be fully explained here, but choices exist among the *term* and *type* of mortgage. Most terms are fifteen or thirty years, with a few at ten and twenty years. The difference in payment between the shorter term and longer term mortgage is not as great as you would think, and the interest cost avoided and faster equity buildup are very attractive for long-term wealth building (as demonstrated in Question 70).

Fixed and *adjustable* are the two primary mortgage types. With a fixed mortgage, interest rates and payments remain unchanged for the life of the mortgage. Adjustable mortgages have different interest rates and different payments depending on the prevailing interest rates. While the interest rate has an upper limit, or "cap," an unfavorable climate can drive your payments much higher. For a 30-year, $300,000 mortgage, a 1 percent increase in rates adds nearly $200 to the payment. Many adjustable mortgages offer low "teaser" rates that may appear attractive today. ARMs can work but are more dangerous in a low interest rate environment because the more likely upward rate trajectory can be hazardous to your finances unless you expect your income to grow—a more dubious proposition in an environment of increasing rates. Opt for the fixed mortgage if you can, unless current interest rates are higher than historic norms.

Question 69: **How big should my mortgage be?**

If possible, you should borrow no more than 80 percent of the value of the home. Why? Because most lenders require *PMI*—private mortgage insurance—to cover the loan should you die or become disabled. PMI adds to the cost of your home and brings little peace of mind other than for the lender.

Some lenders will loan 90 percent, 95 percent, and even higher percentages of *LTV,* or Loan to Value, but this usually brings higher interest rates in addition to PMI. Most people find it more comfortable to put more down and get a smaller mortgage if they can. With today's home equity lines, that additional equity is not as tied up as it once was.

Question 70: **Should I get a thirty-year mortgage or something shorter?**

For a $300,000 mortgage, a thirty-year loan at 6 percent requires a monthly payment of $1,798/month, while the fifteen-year equivalent is $2,531/month. So for an extra $700/month, you can be mortgage-free in fifteen years. Put another way, in fifteen years you will accumulate $300,000 in equity—savings—compared to about $87,000 with the thirty-year mortgage.

The following table, based on the same $300,000 mortgage at 6 percent, shows the difference in payments, total interest paid over the life of the loan, and equity accumulation after ten years. The advantages of shorter loan periods are obvious and should be pursued if income permits. Most mortgage lenders offer slightly preferred rates, ¼ to ½ percent less, for shorter terms.

Mortgage Term	Monthly Payment	Total Interest Paid	Equity after 10 Years
10-year	$3330	$99,600	$300,000
15-year	$2531	$165,300	$169,053
20-year	$2149	$215,700	$106,405
30-year	$1798	$347,000	$48,942

With most mortgages, you can make extra payments to shorten the mortgage, save interest, and increase equity buildup. While pursuing this option can preserve flexibility to handle income shortfalls, many people don't have the discipline to sustain the extra payments.

Question 71: Why are interest rates so important? Do they really make a difference?

We saw in Question 68 how a 1 percent interest rate increase on a $300,000 loan increases the monthly payment by $200. You can interpret this figure for your own situation: if you have a $200,000 loan, the increase will be about two-thirds as much, or about $130. Note that shorter term loans are somewhat less interest-sensitive; the same $300,000 loan payment over fifteen years only increases by $165/month, or about 6.5 percent, for each 1 percent change in the interest rate.

Question 72: **What makes mortgage rates change, and what should I keep track of and why?**

Mortgages are essentially bonds that you *sell*. An investor buys the "bond" from you, loaning you money today with your promise to pay in the future with interest. Therefore, mortgage rates are largely dictated by the bond market—the market for loaned funds. Since mortgages are long-term instruments, the long-term market for loaned funds is most important. Prospective mortgagees should monitor changes in long-term bond rates, particularly ten-year U.S. Treasury bonds and similar instruments.

It is also important to monitor factors that drive these rates. Inflation is the most important driver since it affects the real value of dollars paid back to the lender. High inflation leads to high interest rates, as government policymakers typically use interest rates to control inflation. So factors signaling—or causing—inflation are important, such as raw material prices, strong economic growth, and rising labor costs. In thinking through this, you'll realize that the lowest interest rates are available during weak economic times—which may or may not be when you're ready to buy.

Question 73: **What are the real costs of owning a home?**

Like any asset, one must be aware of the total cost of ownership of a home. The first and most obvious cost is the cost to purchase. Fortunately, the vast majority of homeowners have experienced no decline in value with time or use of the home; in fact, it is quite the opposite. So purchase price usually doesn't figure into the cost of ownership.

However, most people must obtain financing to afford the purchase price, and the cost of this financing is substantial, even with tax benefits. For a $300,000, 6-percent mortgage, you will pay $347,000 in interest over the loan life. Even if you are able to deduct this amount on your taxes—saving possibly 35 percent, it still costs $225,000 of real, earned money, or $7,500/year over the thirty-year period.

The costs don't stop there. Property taxes, on average, run about 1.5 percent of the home's value but can vary a lot depending on location—up to $6,000/year on a $400,000 home on average and to $15,000 or higher in some high-tax locales. Homeowner's insurance may run another $1,000 more in areas prone to crime or natural disasters. After that, the maintenance costs vary according to the home and how you decide to keep it, but you should figure at least 1 percent of the value of the home each year and more if the home is older. In total, these costs usually add up to between 3 and 10 percent of the home's value. This isn't to say you shouldn't own a home, but you should be aware of the costs.

Question 74: **What are closing costs, and how should they be paid?**

Closing costs are normal transaction costs for transferring real estate from the seller to the buyer. They vary by state to a degree but usually include interest adjustments, property tax adjustments, title insurance, escrow fees, and various public and private fees for transaction recording, inspections, and appraisals.

Interest adjustments simply bring interest payments current to the first of the next month, the beginning of the normal monthly mortgage payment cycle. Property tax adjustments are similar except they are adjusted, or prorated, to the first of the next tax period. Title insurance protects you (and the lender) from potential title conflicts. (Did the previous owner indeed own the property? Were there some "liens," claims as loans or otherwise, against it?) Escrow fees are paid to manage the transaction details, exchange of funds, paperwork, and the official closing and recording at the local public agency. Then other fees are added for inspections as required by local law or as negotiated between buyer and seller, and there will be minor recording fees assessed by the county. Some jurisdictions also charge transfer taxes, akin to sales taxes, and many escrow offices will charge fees for document creation and express delivery. The list is long, and you have every right to understand each item.

Typically closing costs are negotiated between the buyer and seller. The seller might pay for escrow, title insurance, and all required inspections while the buyer picks up discretionary inspections and the appraisal. The buyer pays interest and tax adjustments since they will own the property during the adjustment period.

Question 75: **When should I consider refinancing?**

Typically refinancing is considered if (1) you plan to stay in the home for at least five more years and (2) if the interest rate would decline about 2 percent. The decision drivers are closing costs and the size of the mortgage. Do the potential payment savings during the next few years of ownership pay the costs? The decision requires careful calculation of closing costs. Many refinance lenders are picking up some of these costs, making the proposition more attractive. Some homeowners, especially with large mortgages, are finding it attractive to refinance with as little as a 1/2 percent drop in the interest rate. It also makes sense to refinance to move from an ARM to the stability of a fixed rate mortgage.

Question 76: **Should I consider paying off my mortgage early? Why or why not?**

Aside from refinancing, this is one of the most common questions during home ownership, and financial advisors bring wide-ranging opinions to the topic.

The answer, for most, is probably "yes." First among the many principles involved: you should if at all possible pay off your mortgage before retirement, greatly reducing required cash flow.

Paying a mortgage early saves interest cost and puts you in a far more secure and flexible financial position. It's equivalent to buying a bond at the same *coupon*, or interest rate, as the mortgage rate since you are saving that amount of interest. As an investment, this works unless you spend the saved proceeds.

The counterpoint: paying off the house ties up funds in the real estate, denying potentially higher returns available from other investments (like stocks). However, considering risk, the tradeoff may be favorable especially if you have other funds to invest. Others argue that capital tied up in home equity is inaccessible, even for emergencies. The wide availability of home equity credit lines makes this less true.

Today you may still encounter financial advisors recommending against early payoff, but one must suspect motives, as it removes money from their oversight. If other financial needs are met and income is reasonably stable, early payoff makes sense.

Question 77: My friends tell me I should buy rental property. Is this good advice? What do I need to consider?

Rental property has historically been a good investment for most, as rents and property values have both risen steadily. While it may take a while to recover insurance, tax, and maintenance costs through increased rents, eventually it all seems to work out.

However, many people fail to consider *all* of the costs—including time and effort—of maintaining a rental property. For many, taking care of their own home is enough. Now they are in the position of landlord, having to deal with tenants in what is often a stressful situation. Finally, landlords must deal with at least some vacancy. The property will not be rented 100 percent of the time, and some effort and cost will have to go toward replacing tenants from time to time.

Buying a rental property should be looked at like starting a business. What are the potential revenues, costs, and uncertainties? Does it pencil out? Do you have the skills, time, patience, and risk tolerance to run the business? If so, it may be for you.

Chapter 8

PLANNING FOR COLLEGE

For families with children, the cost of college is one of the biggest financial hurdles encountered during a lifetime. Today's job market requires some form of formal education as almost a given. College is expensive to begin with, but costs have escalated relentlessly and are projected to escalate about 6 percent per year. This is double the rate of inflation, but the truly bad news is that state budget problems are driving a projected 10 percent rise in public university tuitions. Planning for college must be done carefully, but, as shown in what follows, there are many ways to do it.

Question 78: **How much do we need to save for college?**

The amount needed to fund a college education depends on the number of children you have, kind of college they might attend, and projected cost increases for that college. There is a big difference between costs of public in-state, public out-of-state, and private colleges. The location also affects living costs; colleges in urban areas cost more. The financial habits and standard of living of your offspring are also important, and don't forget to include transportation cost if something other than on-campus life is intended.

There are good Internet resources available to track current college costs. The College Board Web site *(www.collegeboard.com)* gives current college costs for individual public and private schools. To project these costs forward, enter the appropriate cost growth rate and the number of years before college starts into the compounding formula:

$$\text{Future cost} = \text{Current cost} \times (1 + \text{growth rate})^{\text{number of years}}$$

So a current cost of $7,000/year would grow to $12,535 at a 6 percent growth rate in 10 years ($7000 × $[1.06]^{10}$). To be really precise, you should repeat the calculation for each of the four years to be supported and add the results for a total figure.

Question 79: **What are the main ways to finance college costs?**

The many traditional and creative ways to finance a college education fall into one of three categories:

- *Savings plans* accumulate funds or prepay tuition (a form of savings) usually with favorable tax consequences. Normal household savings and real estate equity figure in, too.
- *Tax relief* goes beyond tax-preferred savings plans with specific credits and tax deductions for college and college-related costs.
- *Financial aid* supplements your savings through a system of grants and loans. Some, but not all, aid is based on need.

The best strategy is to build savings first, then use aid and tax breaks to fill the gaps. People tend to depend too much on financial aid. Instead of saving, they support an excessive standard of living and rely on aid—with lasting negative effects.

Question 80: **What are the best savings alternatives, and how do they work?**

Specialized college savings plans give a tax break on earnings (not original principal) added to an account. In the case of 529 plans, investments are geared toward college savings. The three main types are:

Coverdell IRAs (once known as Educational IRAs) allow a $2,000 annual contribution per child from anyone (it doesn't have to be a parent). These funds can be invested as you wish, and investment gains are tax-free. Household income must be less than $190,000 to make a full contribution. Advantages include investment flexibility; disadvantages include the limited contribution. It's hard to accumulate all college needs at $2,000/year, and you may have to pay someone to manage the investments.

Qualified State Tuition Plans, or QSTPs, come in two forms: Section 529 tuition prepayment plans and college savings trusts. Prepaid tuition plans have been around for some time, while 529 savings plans are relatively new. Both are discussed in more detail later in this chapter.

Educational Savings Bonds are Series I or EE bonds offered by the U.S. Treasury. These bonds are safe. I-bonds have an inflation-indexing feature, but rates are low (3.39 percent for fall 2004). They are state and local tax-exempt and can be federal tax-exempt if used for qualified educational expenses if you are in qualifying tax brackets. For details, see the U.S. Treasury savings bond site (*www.publicdebt.treas.gov*). Series EE bonds are issued at a discount and don't have the inflation protection factor.

Question 81: **I've heard a lot about 529 plans. What are the key features and pros and cons?**

529 savings plans are college savings trusts set up under Section 529 of the Internal Revenue Service code. Within certain guidelines, each state can set up a trust managed by an investment company. (TIAA-CREF is the largest, but there are others.) Investors get some but not a lot of choice of investments—usually conservative equity funds, bond funds, or a self-directed or automatically reallocated mix of the two investments. Earnings (not original contributions) are tax-free. The biggest advantages are the large maximum contribution limit (usually greater than $200,000 per child), automatic payment programs, and special estate planning consideration. There are no income limits, and eligible expenses are broadly defined to include college living expenses. Special estate planning considerations include accelerated gifting, where up to five times the normal $11,000 exclusion can be gifted tax-free per giver per recipient. Retained ownership allows a grandparent donor to set the trust in their name with a grandchild as beneficiary, effectively transferring the assets but retaining control. (If the assets must be retained for use by the elder and not for educational purposes, a 10 percent penalty applies, but this is far less expensive than paying estate or gift taxes.) 529 plans work for all savers and especially wealthy families. Disadvantages include relatively poor investment returns, high fees in some plans, and inflexible investments. The College Savings Plan Network portal (*www. collegesavings.org*) gives a good summary of each state plan.

Question 82: **How do I choose a state for our 529 savings plan?**

Every state has a slightly different plan—different investment advisors, investments, fees, and past performance. You can invest in any state. Choice of state is really a matter of personal preference for investment choices, track record, and fees. Some states offer a *state* income tax preference for funds invested in their own state.

Question 83: **What are the advantages and disadvantages of prepaid tuition plans?**

Prepaid tuition plans are the predecessors of the ever more popular 529 plans. A prepaid plan allows payment of in-state state college tuition at a deep discount well in advance of enrollment, either as a lump sum or a series of regular payments. But not all states offer them, and while generally they can be used for private schools or state schools in other states, there may be strings attached, such as withdrawal fees and forfeited returns. They don't guarantee admission, and they only pay for tuition and fees, not books, living, and transportation expenses. Most prefer the more flexible and expense-inclusive 529 savings plans.

Question 84: **What are the major forms of tax relief for college costs, and how can they help?**

The IRS offers a complex and frequently changing set of tax credits and deductions to help offset some, but not all, college costs. These tools are typically only available for families with adjusted gross income under $130,000 ($65,000 for single parents).

- The *Hope Scholarship Credit* is a tax credit (which is better than a deduction) of up to $1,500/year per student for qualified educational expenses during the first two years of school. Qualified educational expenses only include tuition and fees, not living expenses.
- The *Lifetime Learning Credit* picks up where the Hope Scholarship Credit leaves off, giving a credit of 20 percent of the first $10,000 of qualified expenses for a maximum annual credit of $2,000 per family. Only tuition and fees are covered, but education is defined more broadly to include professional training and seminars.
- Up to $2,500 of *student loan interest* is deductible against income, if income qualifications are met.

For the Hope Scholarship and Lifetime Learning credits, there is a $4,000 cap per year per family.

Question 85: **What are the different kinds of financial aid, and which is best?**

Beyond savings and tax incentives, there are a variety of aid plans. Most are offered or supported by the federal government; some are from states, schools, or private foundations. The two main categories are *grants* and *loans*. Grants aren't paid back and are usually based on need. Loans may or may not be based on need or have different terms depending on need.

Major federal grant programs include Pell and Supplemental Educational Opportunity Grants, which range from a few hundred dollars to $3,000 (Pell) or $4,000 (SEOG) per year. Both consider family need.

Loan programs are extensive and have varied features. Some have preference for students with need. Some loans are made to students, and some loans are made to parents. Some loans are for undergraduates, while other loans cover graduate students or both. Most have favorable interest rates and payment terms.

- *Perkins loans* are targeted toward families with high need and can finance up to $20,000 (undergraduate) or $40,000 (graduate) in expenses at a maximum interest rate of 5 percent with payments deferred until after graduation.
- *Stafford loans* are made to students and provide increasing amounts as the student progresses through college. They may be *subsidized* (lower interest rates qualified by need) or *unsubsidized*. Loan limits are high, up to $10,500/year for undergraduate students and $18,500/year for graduate students. Interest rates cannot exceed 8.5 percent. A disadvantage: these loans are made through private institutions (banks), which may charge hefty origination fees.
- *Parent Loans to Undergraduate Students* (PLUS) loans are made to parents and have variable interest rates, not to exceed 9 percent. These loans can originate at private institutions or directly through the U.S. Department of Education. Balances are limited only by education cost and may be paid off in part through public service.

Question 86: **How "poor" do we have to be to qualify for financial aid?**

The financial aid process is complex, but it usually starts with submitting a standard form known as the Free Application for Federal Student Aid (FAFSA). The form details family assets and income, and financial aid officers determine an *EFC*, or Expected Family Contribution, from the data supplied. The formula is complex, but it considers a combination of assets, income, age, number of children, and special financial circumstances. Primary residences, farms, and retirement plans are generally excluded. A rule of thumb: a parent might be expected to supply on average, depending on income, 10 to 12 percent of net assets, while a student might be expected to supply 35 percent of net assets. (So don't give too much to the student in advance.) The percentage climbs fast as family income increases. Further details are available in the *College Costs and Financial Aid Handbook* published by the College Entrance Examination Board.

Question 87: **What's the downside of student loans?**

Many families depend on student loans as the solution to get them through college costs requirements. But beware: debt is debt. Whether obtained by the student or parent, these loans need to be paid off. Five or ten years of debt payments by newly employed students can set back their finances and savings plans. Wouldn't it be better to start their retirement savings early with forty years of compounding? As for the parent, payments could instead go to retirement preparation—paying off the mortgage, for instance. While interest rates are capped, they are still high by 2004–2005 standards. Loan fees, especially for Stafford loans, can be expensive.

Question 88: **Should I borrow against my home equity to finance college?**

When college requirements arrive, many families find their biggest asset and source of cash is the equity in their homes. Should they borrow against it for college? Home equity loan interest rates and probable interest tax deductibility are attractive. Obtaining the loan is easy and is devoid of cost if the credit line is already set up. While these pros are attractive, it really depends on the state of other retirement assets. If retirement is sufficiently funded elsewhere, tapping home equity might be sound. However, if retirement is a question mark, home equity (and other assets, to the extent possible) should be preserved. Why? Any advisor will tell you that you can borrow elsewhere for college, but you can't borrow for retirement.

Question 89: **Given all the tools, what is the best strategy for meeting college needs?**

Whether you are of high, low, or average means, planning for college takes commitment and creativity to effectively use the strategies and tools available. People of modest means are advised to make full use of available tax breaks, loans, and grants. This means keeping up with the rules and watching the costs and aid policies of chosen colleges. Even a trickle going into savings plans—Coverdell or 529—makes sense and is easy, particularly with 529 monthly payment plans. These plans effectively employ a "dollar cost averaging" approach and have the potential to make a big dent over the long run. A monthly deposit of $50 made over fifteen years, assuming a 6 percent investment return, provides $14,540, enough to pay a year or two of college costs (depending on tuition inflation).

Wealthier families might lose some of the tax breaks and preferential loan treatment, but they can make full use of the 529 savings plans, especially in the estate plans of elder family members. The gifting rules for 529s make it extraordinarily easy to transfer assets to other family members—for a good cause—while still preserving ownership and control and enjoying tax-free growth and compounding.

Chapter 9

PLANNING FOR RETIREMENT

Retirement planning is the development of a financial plan to cover your "golden years," where your ability—and willingness—to work for income declines. Retirement planning used to be simple—turn sixty-five, collect Social Security and an employer pension, move to Florida or California, and live happily ever after. Just like about everything else, that's all changed. The age sixty-five cutoff is no longer a given. Many people want to retire or semi-retire early, and many people intend to stay active and work longer. "Automatic" pensions are disappearing in favor of self-built and self-directed retirement assets. Earned income is replaced with income from your assets, and how that happens is your responsibility. The bottom line: retirement planning has become both more complex and more important.

Question 90: **Every day I read about the importance of retirement planning. Why has it become such a big issue?**

Put simply, you need more at a time when you're guaranteed less. You're likely to live longer, retire earlier (or at least want to), and want a higher standard of living during retirement. You want to take vacations, visit distant grandchildren, and live comfortably. At the same time, employers are dropping guaranteed pensions, Social Security is gradually reducing benefits, and financial assets are more volatile. The replacement of defined retirement benefits with self-directed retirement plans is one big manifestation of this trend.

Question 91: **What are the major elements of a retirement plan?**

Retirement plans have three main parts:

- *Total needs analysis* addresses how much will be needed over what period of time. The first step is deciding how long you are likely to live, and the second step is projecting the standard of living you aspire to.
- Determining *entitlements* is the second part of planning. What "guaranteed" benefits are you entitled to? Social Security is most common, but pensions and other annuities are also considered.
- *Net needs analysis* subtracts entitlements from total needs; this is what you need to provide in the form of savings. The amount depends on time until retirement and investment return assumptions.

Question 92: **How do I determine my total needs for retirement? Are there any factors I can control?**

Total needs is based on length of life after retirement and the standard of living desired. Length of life is an educated guess at best (and don't forget to include your spouse). Today's life expectancy requires planning for at least twenty years; many look out to twenty-five to thirty years and naturally more if they plan to retire early.

The next step is estimating income required to support your standard of living. Most need 70 to 80 percent of their gross income when working. This can vary depending on health, whether your home is paid for, and more generally the retirement lifestyle you want to live. If you want to travel overseas each year and make three cross-country trips per year to visit grandkids, plan for more. If retirement includes a motor home, boat, or new car every three years, plan for more. Make a list of what will be cheaper and what will be more expensive. Conservative planners use 100 percent of income as an assumption, giving a cushion if nothing else.

Question 93: **Suppose I decide, after total needs and entitlement analysis, that I need $3,000/month for thirty years of retirement to achieve my desired standard of living. How do I convert that into an amount to save?**

Once you determine monthly retirement income need and time duration, simple *distribution annuity* math gives the amount you will need to save. (You can find a further explanation of this concept on page 57 of *The Everything® Personal Finance Book* [Adams Media, 2003], by this author.) A distribution annuity is a sum of money capable of paying a fixed amount per month while keeping retained funds invested at a given rate of return. It is not a product you buy (although it can be) but rather a mathematical calculation.

The following table (presented previously in the answer to Question 21) gives the mathematical factors you need to make a calculation of how much you will have to save. At an assumed 7 percent return on retained investments, the annual mathematical factor for thirty years is 12.4. So take your monthly stipend, annualize it ($36,000), and multiply by 12.4. The result is $446,400 to be saved. However, this assumes zero inflation. If you assume 3 percent inflation over the period, "real" investment return is reduced to 4 percent. The factor for 4 percent is 17.3, increasing the savings needed to $622,800. Yes, inflation does make a difference.

Distribution Annuity Table

Interest	Number of Years							
Rate %	1	2	5	10	15	20	30	40
4.0%	1.0	1.9	4.5	8.1	11.1	13.6	17.3	19.8
5.0%	1.0	1.9	4.3	7.7	10.4	12.5	15.4	17.2
6.0%	0.9	1.8	4.2	7.4	9.7	11.5	13.8	15.0
7.0%	0.9	1.8	4.1	7.0	9.1	10.6	12.4	13.3
8.0%	0.9	1.8	4.0	6.7	8.6	9.8	11.3	11.9
10.0%	0.9	1.7	3.8	6.1	7.6	8.5	9.4	9.8
12.0%	0.9	1.7	3.6	5.7	6.8	7.5	8.1	8.2
15.0%	0.9	1.6	3.4	5.0	5.8	6.3	6.6	6.6
20.0%	0.8	1.5	3.0	4.2	4.7	4.9	5.0	5.0

Question 94: With regard to Social Security, how much income can you count on?

Social Security is set up to provide about 24 percent of your preretirement income, more for lower earners, less for higher earners. To determine your exact payment, Social Security uses a complex formula to calculate your *Average Indexed Monthly Earnings* (AIME) at retirement. Based on the latest figures for 2005, your payment is then based on 90 percent of the first $592 of AIME, 32 percent of the next $2,975, and then 15 percent of the amount over $3,567, up to a maximum monthly benefit of $1,874 for age sixty-five retirees. So if your salary at retirement is $60,000 and your AIME works out to $5,000/month, you will receive $1,699.75/month, or about 34 percent of preretirement income. Your exact payment will vary according to your AIME, which in turn varies according to your income history, so it is difficult to calculate your *exact* payment using your current annual income. Note that Social Security, through changes in the formula and retirement ages, intends to lower the average preretirement percentage to about 20 percent. Regardless of change, the need for income beyond Social Security is obvious.

Question 95: **I worked all my life, and my spouse stayed at home and only worked sporadically. How much Social Security will we get? What if I pass away?**

The general rule is that spouses get the larger of their own entitled Social Security payment or one-half of your payment when they reach eligible retirement age. So if you're entitled to $1,540/month based on your AIME and retirement age and your spouse is entitled to $950, you would get a combined total of $2,490/month. If the spouse was only eligible for $650 based on his or her earnings, you would receive $2,260/month ($1540 × 1.5).

If you die or your spouse is disabled or there are dependent children involved, the scenario changes considerably. In the case of death of the primary earner, payments are available for dependent children ($1,037/month in the previous example), and the spousal payment would increase to $1,380/month.

Question 96: **I was born in 1956. What are my retirement options, and how do they affect my Social Security payout?**

Your choices boil down to early, full, and deferred retirement. Recent Social Security changes increased the full retirement age for those born after 1937, scaling gradually upward from sixty-five to sixty-seven years if born in 1960 or later. Early retirement can start at age sixty-two. If you were born in 1956, full retirement can start at age sixty-six years, four months, and deferred retirement starts beyond sixty-six years, four months.

Aside from the effects of a premature death, when you retire has nothing to do with how much total Social Security you get. It only affects when you get it. Early retirees simply spread their payments out over a longer period so that the payment is reduced. Deferred retirees forgo payment in years sixty-two to seventy so that there is more available once they start to draw. The following table illustrates this (based on 2004 figures).

Retirement age	Salary $50,000	Salary $100,000
62	$1,108/month	$1,461/month
66 years, 4 months	$1,545/month	$2,015/month
70 years	$2,027/month	$2,639/month

Premature death is the problem with waiting longer. If you die at age seventy-two, you'll only receive two years of the higher payment; payments you would have received for years sixty-two to seventy are lost forever. The Social Security Administration Web site has a basic benefits calculator (*www.ssa.gov*) to estimate your options.

Question 97: **I divorced my husband twenty years ago. To what, if any, Social Security am I entitled?**

Generally, if you were married ten years or more and have not remarried, you're eligible for benefits using the standard spousal formula, that is, the greater of your eligible benefits or one-half of your spouse's benefit. It gets more complicated if you are disabled or have a dependent child under sixteen living with you; generally you get more and are eligible sooner, at age sixty in most cases. The formulas are complex; you're best advised to contact the nearest Social Security Administration office directly. They are typically helpful. The Social Security Administration publishes an excellent summary entitled "What Every Woman Should Know" covering this and other issues, at *www.ssa.gov/pubs/10127.html*.

Question 98: **My income isn't very high now, not enough to cover both college and retirement needs. What should I focus on?**

With the trend toward getting married and having children later and later in life, this is the common conundrum faced by more people in middle age. Many just saved money without considering the dual needs of college and retirement and find themselves facing college expenses—then retirement expenses just a few years later.

When faced with this dilemma, retirement should get primary focus. Why? Simply because nobody will lend you money for retirement. It is possible to borrow money for a college education (see Chapter 8), and it is even plausible for our children to pay for some or all of college, either now or eventually. But once precious retirement resources are committed to college, they are hard to replace, especially in a short time frame. So the best advice is to save for both if possible, but to prioritize retirement.

Question 99: **Scenario: I was born in 1956 and plan to retire at age sixty-six years, four months, earning about $50,000/year. My spouse will retire two years later with earnings of about $25,000. Can we run a rough calculation of what I need to save?**

First, let's simplify the calculation by assuming your spouse will retire at the same time. Put another way, we'll calculate what you need going forward after he or she retires. Based on the Questions 95 and 96 (using 2004 figures) we can estimate your Social Security receipts at $1,545/month. Your spouse will be eligible for $1,008/month (90 percent of $531 + 32 percent of $1,552). Since that is greater than one-half of your amount, your total monthly Social Security payment will be $2,553.

Now your standard of living today is based on $75,000 annual income. Make the assumption you want, but let's suppose you can live on 80 percent of that amount, or $60,000/year. That's $5,000/month.

So Social Security provides about half; you must come up with $2,447/month after any applicable taxes to meet your desired standard of living, or $29,364/year. What amount of money, if deposited today, would provide $29,364/year? Let's make it an even $35,000/year to give room to pay taxes, handle emergencies, etc.

Using distribution annuity math, assuming twenty years of life in retirement and a 4 percent net return after inflation, the factor is 13.6. Multiply 13.6 by $35,000, and you get $476,900 in savings at retirement day one required to sustain your lifestyle after Social Security.

Question 100: **What are the different employer retirement plans available? Can you summarize?**

Retirement plans and the pension and tax law that sits behind them are very complex and beyond the scope of most workers. Many specialized retirement plan forms were set up for small business, professional corporations like doctors and lawyers, and the self-employed. For most normal wage earners, retirement plans fall into one of two camps: *defined benefit* and *defined contribution* plans. In defined benefit plans, the employer commits to the benefit and takes responsibility to make it happen. Defined contribution plans define the contribution, not the benefit. The benefit is based on what's in the plan at retirement. The popular IRAs are individual plans, not employer plans.

Traditional pensions are defined benefit plans. Pensions give what was promised, and the company is legally obligated to deposit enough funds into the plan to make it happen. The risks of investment performance and earning the funds to deposit are all borne by the employer, but the employer does receive the tax benefit.

Defined contribution plans are mainly either *profit sharing* or so-called *salary reduction* plans. Profit sharing plans have a promised pay-in based on a percentage of profits, but no guaranteed pay-in or benefit; they are mainly designed to defer taxes. Profit sharing plans must be equitable; that is, they don't prefer the higher-level employees. Salary reduction plans allow you to set aside income on a pretax basis, with possible employer match. The popular 401(k) is an example.

Most notably, defined contribution plans shift all retirement funding risk to you. What you accumulate depends on what is contributed and how it is invested. There is no guarantee or obligation for the employer to pay a retirement benefit. As a consequence, the trend today is toward defined contribution plans, shifting responsibility to you. The ramifications shouldn't be overlooked.

Question 101: **I have a pension plan. Is there anything to worry about?**

The benefit promise provided by a traditional pension plan is certainly attractive as today's retirement plans move away from guaranteed benefits. However, as seen in industries like steel and airlines, even a pension is not completely secure if the employer fails in business. Although bankruptcy courts put a high priority on pension pay-outs, it is possible for a company to terminate or reduce a pension plan in bankruptcy, or they may underfund it along the way, making eventual bankruptcy and default more likely. The good news: the government-backed *Pension Benefit Guarantee Corporation* (PBGC) stands behind pensions in much the same way as the *Federal Deposit Insurance Corporation* (FDIC) stands behind bank and savings and loan deposits. This helps, but there is growing concern that even PBGC won't be able to meet all obligations. Finally, you should pay attention to annual company pension statements to make sure expected payouts are keeping pace with inflation.

Keep tabs on the business affairs of your employer, and don't depend too much on the pension. You can build other retirement savings with IRAs—Roth IRAs are probably best—and through normal savings and real estate equity buildup. One other thing—pensions may be guaranteed, but health benefits are *not*. Many companies are cutting back in this important area.

Question 102: **Are retirement savings plans tax-free?**

The short answer is "no." Whether they are employer plans (pension, profit sharing, salary reduction) or individual (IRAs), most retirement savings plans defer taxes; they don't eliminate them completely. That is, tax may be deferred on funds paid in, causing a short-term reduction in tax liability. But the eventual withdrawal of those funds is taxable. The good news: most are in a lower tax bracket in retirement, so the tax bite is less. With that said, many people forget to incorporate taxes into their retirement planning needs. The funds you withdraw will be taxable.

The notable exception is Roth IRAs. Roth IRAs are funded with after-tax dollars so that deposited funds can be withdrawn tax-free—in fact at any time, preretirement or postretirement. More importantly, the earnings on funds in the account *are also* tax-free. This tax advantage combined with the unlimited account retention (that is, no mandatory withdrawals at age seventy-and-a-half), make Roth IRAs a powerful long-term savings tool.

Question 103: **I plan to leave my current position. What are my retirement plan options, and which is best?**

If you have been with your employer long enough with enough in your retirement plan, you have a choice to leave your retirement plan intact or to "roll it over" into another. The rollover rules are fairly complex, but in general, you can roll over any type of plan (profit sharing plan, 401[k] plan, lump sum cashout of a pension plan) into a traditional or Roth IRA. Generally you have sixty days to complete the rollover. There is some paperwork. It is not too complex, and most receiving financial institutions will gladly assist you.

Assuming you're eligible to keep the plan intact, the rollover choice is mainly a matter of personal preference. Many prefer to consolidate their retirement savings into a single plan, rather than scattering about bits and pieces. Rollover IRAs have more investment options; you aren't constrained by investment choices as in the employer plan. You may encounter modest fees in the rollover account, but in general there is no cost penalty. Note that you cannot reverse the rollover should you decide to return to that employer.

Question 104: **My company retirement plan has an option to take a lump sum at retirement or convert to an annuity. Which is better?**

A tough choice with no guiding rule, this decision depends on your preferences and payout features.

Lump sum distributions cash you out at a calculated accrued value of your plan. Pension plans do not have assets individually tagged with your name on them; they are a shared pool of assets. So the assumptions used to determine your portion are important. A lump sum must be rolled over into another retirement vehicle (to avoid paying taxes on a singular high amount). How you invest the proceeds becomes important. Depending on the plan, buying an annuity on the open market might be attractive but be careful about high commissions.

Annuity payouts are attractive for those expecting to live a long life (especially if it's a *joint and survivor annuity* covering your spouse at your death, that is, two people have to die to cease payment). At the end of the day, it's a complex pros and cons analysis, so it's best to take your time, analyze payout alternatives closely, and get professional help.

Question 105: **How do 401(k) plans work, and why is everybody so positive about them?**

A *401(k)* plan is a salary deferral plan, where a certain percentage of your salary can be set aside before taxes in a company-sponsored investment plan. The main attractions are the relatively large amount that can be set aside (for 2005, 17 percent of salary up to $14,000/ year), and many companies match your deferral up to 3 percent of your salary. The combination of large contributions, company match, and tax-deferred growth can be powerful; with moderate investment success, it is possible for average earners to accumulate $1 million or more in these plans. For example, a wage earner (or husband/wife combination) earning $80,000/year and setting aside 10 percent with a 3 percent employer match ($10,400/year), with a 7 percent return over thirty years (an accumulation annuity factor of 94.1), accumulates $978,640 at the end of the thirty years.

The high growth potential is attractive to employees, and shifting investment risk to the employee and administrative simplicity are attractive to the employer, hence the recent popularity. But employees accept the risk, and investment choices, which may be limited in some plans, are enormously important.

Question 106: **How much can I contribute to my 401(k)?**

After remaining constant for many years, the IRS is gradually increasing annual contribution limits. As mentioned previously, for 2005 the limit is 17 percent of salary up to a maximum of $14,000/year (up from

$11,000 in 2002); it is scheduled to rise to $15,000 by 2006 and be adjusted for inflation thereafter. A special provision allows earners age fifty and over to defer an extra $3,000/year, rising to $5,000/year in 2006. On the Web, *www.401khelpcenter.com* is a good resource to monitor 401(k) rules.

Question 107: My employer offers a series of 401(k) investment choices. How should I allocate my investments? Should I rotate them actively?

Particularly considering tax-deferred returns, 401(k) investing choices can have a major impact on future wealth. Employers usually outsource the management of 401(k) plans to a plan administrator; the administrator offers a series of investment choices with employer agreement. These choices usually consist of a series of mutual funds, often a set of in-house administrator funds, Fidelity being a common example. The funds cover a range of investment classes from large cap stocks to international to bond funds. Usually there is an offering tracking the shares of the employer if publicly traded. The variety of funds offered has increased in recent years, driven in part by concerns about mutual funds and overexposure to a limited few investments.

There are no set investing guidelines; however, it does make sense, given tax deferral and the long-term nature of these plans, to weight toward growth-oriented investments. Thirty years in a short-term bond or money market fund won't achieve your investing objectives, although it might be a good safe haven at times. Most advisors recommend staying the course, not doing too much switching, and avoiding overweight—more than 20 to 30 percent of holdings—in the company's own shares.

Question 108: I've heard you can't withdraw funds from a 401(k) plan before age 59½ without incurring a 10 percent penalty. What are the exceptions?

Generally, this rule is right, but there are some "hardship exceptions":

- Involuntary job termination beyond age fifty-five
- Unreimbursed medical costs exceeding 7.5 percent of adjusted gross income
- Divorce agreement shifting funds to spouse or dependent
- Total disability
- Death and transfer of account to beneficiary

Question 109: **What should I look for in a good 401(k) plan?**

The best 401(k) plans have immediate eligibility, generous employee match, easy administration (including account balance tracking, investment changes, etc.), and quality investment choices. There should be at least ten to twelve investment choices available; more is better. Choices should run the range from money market and bond funds to conservative and aggressive equity funds and should include "name brand" mutual fund choices. Expenses should be low (less than 1 percent) or, better yet, paid by the employer. Better 401(k) plans have advisors available by telephone (usually employed by the plan administrator) to help with your investment choices and administrative issues.

Question 110: **I want to buy a home, and I have heard that I can borrow against my 401(k) plan to do so. Can I, and is it a good idea?**

Loans against 401(k) accounts are generally allowed by law but may be restricted or disallowed by your employer. Most 401(k) plans allow borrowing of up to 50 percent of the vested balance at a plan-specified interest rate to be paid back in five years. Many plans limit loans and can be only for qualified educational or medical expenses or to purchase a home. Attractively, interest paid goes into your account, not to a lender, and such loans avoid the 10 percent withdrawal penalty.

Should 401(k) loans be used to buy a home? Probably not. While interest is recaptured into your own account, the rate is usually higher. Most loans are due in five years, so it fails as a long-term financing solution. More importantly, assets committed to the loan are pulled out of the investment pool, so you lose long-term growth and compounding on these assets. Finally, balances are due in full upon termination (or else it becomes taxable income), bringing a nasty "double whammy" to your finances, a risk most shouldn't take. If it requires your 401(k) to buy a home, reevaluate the purchase.

Question 111: I am a schoolteacher, and we have a 403(b) plan. Is this different from a 401(k)? How?

403(b) plans are salary deferral plans—much like 401(k)s—that are set up for use by not-for-profit entities such schools, hospitals, public welfare agencies, and churches and church-affiliated organizations. Closely related 457 plans cover many state and local government workers. The popular 401(k) plan actually descended from the 403(b).

Once hatched, 401(k) plans evolved faster, allowing greater deferrals and investment choices. But recent law changes have let 403(b) plans evolve to offer many of the same provisions, including deferral limits and catch-up contributions for fifty-plus earners. There is still another catch-up provision offered to certain employees with fifteen years of service, not available in 401(k)s. Traditional 403(b) plans limited investments to tax-deferred annuities; most now offer ordinary mutual funds. Like 401(k)s, 403(b) plans can be rolled over into other retirement plans at termination.

Question 112: How much can I/we contribute to an IRA?

For many years, annual IRA contributions were limited to $2,000. But attempts to bolster individual retirement saving have triggered a series of increases.

For tax years 2002–04, contributions to all types of individual IRAs, including Roth IRAs, rose to $3,000. That limit rises to $4,000 for 2005–2007, and to $5,000 for 2008 and beyond. Additionally, beyond 2009 there is a provision to increase limits according to an inflation index. Catch-up contributions allow another $500 each year for age fifty-plus workers.

Besides these limits, there are also maximum compensation limits for certain IRAs. For Roth IRAs, full contributions are allowed up to a maximum compensation of $150,000, phasing out completely at $160,000. There are also income limits and conditions to be satisfied to make traditional IRAs *deductible*—see Question 113 for more on this. There are no compensation limits for *nondeductible* traditional IRAs.

Question 113: **What's the difference between a deductible and a nondeductible IRA? When are IRAs deductible?**

Traditional IRAs are unconditionally deductible—that is, you can deduct your annual contribution for income tax purposes if you don't participate in some other employer-sponsored plan. If an employee participates in a retirement plan (e.g., pension, profit sharing, 401[k] or other salary deferral), the IRS allows deductible IRAs only if the employee falls below certain income limits. In 2005, the limit is $50,000 with a phaseout at $60,000 for single filers. Employees earning over $60,000 cannot deduct traditional IRA contributions but can still make them. For married couples both participating in employer plans, the phaseout begins at $70,000 and ends at $80,000, with higher limits for the nonworking spouse of a participating employee (see Question 114). Remember that Roth IRAs are never deductible.

Question 114: **What is a spousal IRA?**

Recent legislation made it attractive to set up spousal IRAs, that is, IRAs for nonworking spouses of wage earners participating in their employers' plans. Without this provision, unemployed persons were generally not allowed to contribute to IRAs.

Spousal provisions allow a full additional contribution ($4,000 in 2005, rising to $5,000 in 2008) for any spouse as long as returns are filed as "married filing jointly," combined compensation does not exceed $160,000 ($150,000 phaseout), and the IRA is set up in their own account. If the spouse works but doesn't participate in an employer-sponsored plan (see Question 113), the $160,000 limit still applies. If the spouse does participate in an employer-sponsored plan, the joint compensation limit drops to $80,000 in 2005 (with a phaseout beginning at $70,000). As with all IRAs, contributions cannot exceed gross income reported on the return.

Spousal IRAs can be a powerful and often overlooked tool to shelter more income and build still more retirement savings in many households. It also provides a degree of financial security to the nonworking spouse.

Question 115: What is a Roth IRA, and how is it better than a traditional IRA?

Roth IRAs are generally more powerful long-term savings tools for three main reasons:

1. *Tax-free investment income.* Earnings on traditional IRAs—whether contributions are deducted or not—are *tax-deferred;* that is, they are taxable when withdrawn (usually during retirement). Roth earnings are tax *free*—period.
2. *Contributions (not earnings) can be withdrawn at any time* tax- and penalty-free since they were made with after-tax dollars.
3. *No required distributions.* While one must start withdrawing (and paying taxes) from traditional IRAs by age seventy-and-a-half, there is no such requirement for Roth IRAs. Unused funds can be retained to grow further for later retirement years or to pass to heirs. Further, contributions can continue indefinitely, while traditional IRA contributions must stop at age seventy-and-a-half. Finally, accounts transferred to heirs at death are not taxable income. So Roth IRAs are a better tool to build family wealth.

Roth IRA contributions can be made even if participating in an employer-sponsored plan (up to a $150,000 to $160,000 income limit). They can also be added to traditional IRA contributions, subject to the $4,000 (2005–2007) total annual contribution limit.

Generally, one should first contribute to employer-sponsored plans (such as a 401[k]) to enjoy employer contributions and match. Roth IRAs are a good place to put savings beyond family emergency funds and other accessible savings.

Question 116: **Our combined family income exceeds $170,000. Can we and should we still contribute to an IRA?**

You can't contribute to a Roth IRA because of the $160,000 compensation limit, and you can't deduct a traditional IRA contribution if participating in an employer-sponsored plan. That said, a nondeductible traditional IRA is still a good idea, for it sets savings aside and is tax-deferred. So if other savings needs are met, including contributions to company-sponsored plans made so as to fully maximize company match, nondeductible traditional IRAs are still a good idea.

Question 117: **Where should I keep and invest my IRA assets?**

Today, every financial institution offers some form of IRA account, and many offer an assortment. Banks, credit unions, mutual funds, and traditional and discount brokerages are all active in the IRA space.

As an IRA owner, you have a choice between managed and self-directed IRA accounts. Managed accounts have professional managers directing your investments. Most mutual fund companies offer managed accounts, and brokers and now some banks offer them, too. As the name implies, you pay fees for this service, from $50/year to 1 percent of asset amount, depending on the size of the account and the level of management activity. Minimum account sizes may get in the way for some.

Self-directed accounts are set up so that you choose and manage the investments. Such accounts are most often found at discount brokers. Most accounts have a small annual fee (usually $50 or less), although many now waive that fee with a modest minimum balance. Some may have closing fees, and be sure to check the transaction commission rate. Many providers charge higher commissions than for regular "street" accounts, and many will give you a discounted commission on your IRA if you have a traditional street account with them.

As with most investment services, shop to understand services and costs and pick what's right for you. Don't pay for what you don't need.

Question 118: **What kinds of investments can I use for an IRA, and which investments are best?**

By definition, IRAs are long-term investments, and success is driven by steadily compounding growth over a long period of time. When one has many years before retirement, it makes sense to take a little more risk to achieve higher growth rates. When one approaches retirement, one should get more conservative so as to preserve assets in the event of a downturn. As a result, many investors choose to invest more aggressively during their most active working years, gradually shifting investments to more conservative vehicles in the ten years or so before retirement. A convenient rule of thumb used by many: subtract your age from 100—that is the percentage of your IRA (or other retirement account) to invest aggressively.

IRA rules allow investment in almost anything except life insurance and collectibles. Most invest in some combination of individual stocks, mutual funds, and exchange traded funds. Again, steady performance is good, and since all taxes are deferred, the tax characteristics of a fund do not matter. It makes no sense to invest in tax-free vehicles (such as municipal bonds). Most fixed income investments, like CDs or money market funds, don't pay enough to stay ahead of inflation.

During the wealth-accumulation years, steady-performing stocks and growth-oriented mutual funds with low management fees are usually considered best. For the most part, these investments should be left alone to perform and grow (if they can't be, you may have the wrong investment).

Question 119: **I am most comfortable with real estate investments. Do IRAs and other retirement plans allow direct real estate investments?**

Many people feel that real estate is the best long-term investment. Long-term performance is attractive, and many people find it more understandable than business assets. That said—and somewhat surprisingly—it is relatively difficult to place your retirement assets in real estate.

Direct real estate investments (and investments in collectibles and other tangibles as well) are generally not allowed in 401(k) and similar company-sponsored plans. You cannot buy the house next door for your 401(k). However, some securitized real estate investments are allowed, such as real estate investment trusts (REITs). Check to see if your employer-sponsored plan offers REIT investments and then evaluate the REIT carefully.

Technically, all forms of real estate are allowed for IRAs, including direct ownership and limited partnerships. (Many securities brokers offering IRAs don't want you to know this.) But you cannot borrow money to fund an IRA; so you must have enough assets to buy the property outright. The rules are complex; normally such accounts are managed by specialized administrators with high fees. Most individuals use REITs to gain real estate exposure.

Question 120: **I am self-employed. What retirement plans are available, and how do I choose the best one?**

The short answer: self-employed people have more options to choose from than typical employees, and more income can probably be deferred into the plan. The four mainstream choices are SEP IRAs, SIMPLE plans, Keogh plans, and individual IRAs. A quick overview follows.

> *SEP IRAs* are powerful tools that allow you to save up to 25 percent of your draw from the business, up to $41,000/year. They are set up and managed similarly to individual IRAs, but the plan must also include employees (not a problem if you have none).

SIMPLE, or Savings Incentive Match Plans for Employees, allow a relatively large employee contribution ($9,000 or $10,500 if you are fifty or older) per year plus an "employer" (up to 3 percent) match. SIMPLE plans are good if you have employees, for most of the contribution comes from the employee's own salary deferral.

Keogh plans are relatively complex but allow many forms of defined contribution and defined benefit plans, including profit sharing, "money purchase" (where a predetermined amount is to be set aside), and traditional pensions. They are best where many employees and careful financial planning are involved and professional administration is justified.

Finally, *individual IRAs* can be used by self-employed people, either for simplicity where modest contributions are desired ($4,000/year for 2005–2007 plus catch-up provisions), or as "dessert"—to add more to an existing retirement arrangement. Roth IRAs are popular add-ons.

The choices are complex; talk to a financial or tax professional before choosing.

Question 121: Is there a time where I must withdraw from my IRAs? When, how much, and what taxes?

Traditional IRA rules require a minimum distribution before April 1 of the year following attainment of age seventy-and-a-half. The minimum amount is governed by a set of factors corresponding to each year of age from seventy on. For example, the factor for age seventy is 26.2, declining to 25.3 for age seventy-one, 24.4 for age seventy-two, and so forth. The required distribution is calculated by dividing the amount in the plan by the factor; thus the owner of a $500,000 IRA must take a $19,084 distribution ($500,000/26.2) at age seventy, $19,008 at age seventy-one ($480,916/25.3), etc. A stiff 50 percent of the calculated amount is applied as penalty to distributions required but not taken.

If the IRA was a deductible IRA, the entire amount is taxable at the recipient's current income tax rate. If nondeductible, only the earnings are taxable. The Roth IRA provides the happy exception. First, no distribution is required at all; second, all distributions are tax-free.

Question 122: **When do my Social Security benefits become taxable, and how much tax will I pay?**

The rules are fairly complex and are designed to recapture taxes on Social Security received beyond a certain amount of ordinary income. So if you are living on Social Security only, you won't be taxed.

If you are married and earn more than $32,000 ($25,000 single), including one-half of your Social Security benefits and otherwise nontaxable bond interest (yes, it's complicated), your Social Security benefits may be taxed. The percentage of the Social Security that is taxable grows as the adjusted gross income grows. A maximum of 85 percent of your Social Security is taxable at $44,000 joint ($35,000 single) in adjusted income. Income tax is then applied based on your bracket. You don't lose 85 percent of your Social Security, nor do you ever pay tax on 100 percent of it.

Question 123: **What happens if I prematurely withdraw from my IRA or 401(k)?**

Generally, you will pay a 10 percent penalty plus all income taxes due on the taxable portion of your withdrawal before age fifty-nine-and-a-half. For deductible IRAs, this is the entire amount. If you have to take $50,000 from your deductible IRA or 401(k) and are in a 30 percent tax bracket (25 percent federal, 5 percent state), you will pay taxes of $15,000 and a penalty of $5,000—a steep price.

Hardship exceptions are available in IRAs and most 401(k) plans for disability, medical, and educational costs and costs of buying a first home. There is also a *periodic payments provision* set up mainly for prolonged unemployment or early retirement. An equal payment withdrawal over a period of time can be taken from the account without penalty as long as the payment is maintained until age fifty-nine-and-a-half (you must be fifty-five for 401[k]s). Note that these exceptions waive the 10 percent penalty, but funds released are still subject to taxation.

Question 124: **What are annuities, and how do they work?**

Annuities are a hybrid product of investment and insurance, sold like securities by insurance companies. In some ways, they are the reverse of insurance; instead of collecting a periodic premium up-front against a possible payoff, they collect a lump sum up-front against a periodic payout later. Most annuities are set up to buy with a lump sum, often a rollover of retirement assets, to purchase a monthly payment stream for as long as you (and sometimes your spouse) live. Annuity assets grow on a tax-deferred basis, that is, they are allowed to compound without taxation.

The variations and choices among annuity products are vast. You can choose different forms of pay-in, investment, and payout. *Pay-in options* include *immediate* and *deferred*—the payment stream can start immediately, as in retirement, or can start several years later if you're young and want to build savings. The more conservative *fixed annuities* have a fixed payment tied to fixed income securities like bonds, usually with a minimum or "floor" guaranteed by the insurance company. *Variable annuities* have returns tied in part or wholly to a stock market investment portfolio and thus have greater risk.

Payout options are complex. The simplest option gives payments through your lifetime, stopping immediately upon death. But what if you die one month after *annuitizing*—starting—the payment stream? To prevent such a catastrophic loss of assets for your heirs, contracts are written for *periods certain,* that is, a minimum of ten years, twenty years, or other guaranteed payments. Period certain and *joint and survivor* (where your spouse is entitled to continued payments until death) are handy but add to the cost of the annuity.

The chief downside to annuities is the cost. While few charge up-front commissions, many have high surrender charges, up to 10 percent, for up to five, seven, and even ten years after purchase. Fees and expenses can run ½ to 2 percent per year, also a large sum, and there may be other charges. Purchasers must understand all given and potential costs.

Question 125: **How much annuity can you get for your money?**

Even if annuities are not for you, it is useful to think about retirement in annuity terms. What lump sum amount do you need to support a regular retirement income stream? Playing with the numbers is fun and informative; the Web site *www.immediateannuities. com* provides an excellent tool. For instance, in California, a single annuity paying $2,000/month for life starting at age sixty-five costs $313,098. Adding a ten-year period certain raises the cost to $324,123, and adding a joint and survivor provision with a 10-year period certain costs $378,268.

Note that these calculations refer to *immediate annuities*. *Deferred annuities* cost less because they have time to grow. In general, the higher the prevailing interest rates, the lower the initial lump sum required to support a particular payment. Use the Internet to get familiar with annuity products, but then it's a good idea to talk to a professional before buying. The cost of changing your mind can be quite high.

Question 126: **What are the pros and cons of annuities?**

Annuities are a combination of an investment and an insurance policy and combine the advantages and disadvantages of both.
Advantages:

- *Guaranteed payment.* Once an annuity is purchased, a payment is locked in, although the payment might vary depending on the type of annuity. The guarantee makes retirement planning easier
- *Insurance against living too long.* You might plan to live for twenty years in retirement, but what if you live for thirty

years? It's hard to find a job at age eighty-five. Most annuities pay for life—whatever that may be.
- *Tax-deferred returns.* Annuity earnings are taxed only when paid out, usually at lower tax rates.

Disadvantages:

- *High fees and costs,* especially for early surrender.
- *Risk of dying too soon* and not getting full potential payout.
- *Inflation exposure.* A $2,000/month payment might not buy much twenty years from now.
- *Poor investment returns.* Insurance companies must make a profit and generally don't bring the best investment performance, especially considering fees. You may be better off investing on your own (even with mutual funds) and creating your own annuity, but that takes discipline.

Choose carefully and watch out for overdone sales pitches.

Question 127: What are reverse mortgages, and how can I use them in retirement planning?

Relatively new on the retirement planning scene, *reverse mortgages* can be practical for homeowners with substantial home equity who want to stay in their homes. Just as the name suggests, a reverse mortgage pays you, instead of you paying the lender. It can be a regular payment, or it can be managed as a credit line, where you withdraw as needed. As you withdraw, interest is charged on the amount paid to you for the life of the loan. Effectively, the debt on your home grows over time (instead of being reduced). The mortgage is paid off, including the accumulated interest, when the house is sold.

In essence, a reverse mortgage works like an annuity. You pledge an asset—your house—to receive regular payments. There are generally no tax consequences, as payments generally consist of after-tax equity you already own. You must be sixty-two to get a reverse mortgage, and there are limits to what you can borrow. For example, an owner of a $250,000 home can get a thirty-year reverse mortgage tied to $200,000 equity (the current maximum is about $290,000 for any home value), which produces a monthly payment of about $600 with a monthly adjustable interest rate. The National Reverse Loan Mortgage Association provides a good calculator at *www.reversemortgage.org,* and more general information is available from AARP *(www.aarp.org/revmort).* The terms are complex and beware of high fees on loan origination.

Question 128: **Can you summarize retirement planning and saving strategy?**

Like all personal finance, successful retirement planning requires fundamental awareness, commitment, and control. Retirement plans should be carefully established, followed, and monitored for success. A few specific strategies include:

- *Take advantage of available savings plans.* There is a wide array of individual and employer-sponsored plans, many of which can be used in combination. Increased contribution limits have made them more powerful recently.
- *Contribute as much as you can.* The tax-deferred—and sometimes tax-free—status of savings plans is extremely attractive, especially if an employer match is available. Such ability to leverage savings is rare elsewhere.
- *Manage retirement assets actively.* Get the best returns available with a risk you can tolerate; don't just throw it into a low-paying CD or money market fund. In retirement plans, the compounding concept enjoys no finer hour.
- *Pay off your mortgage.* It makes a big difference (1) not having to fund this debt and (2) being able to use home equity for retirement. It also makes a reverse mortgage or "downsizing"—selling the home and buying an annuity with the proceeds—possible.

■ *Plan to supplement retirement income.* A small amount of income from a job or part-time consulting work goes a long way to stretch retirement assets; the mental activity and busy-ness helps in other ways, too.

Question 129: **Scenario: I am fifty and know I've put off saving for retirement. I just spent a lot on sending my children to school. My income is $85,000/year, but I only have $25,000 in retirement savings. I live in a $100,000 home with a $60,000 mortgage. What should I do?**

It's obvious that you're behind in your retirement savings.

The first step is to calculate your gross retirement needs. Living on 75 percent of current gross income would require $5,312/month in retirement. Estimating Social Security benefits is next. At current income levels, the Social Security Administration estimates my benefit at about $1,650/month, leaving a net monthly need of $3,662/month. Assuming a 20-year retirement and an investment return of 6 percent, the distribution annuity factor of 11.8 (See Distribution Annuity Table on page 20) indicates a required lump sum at retirement of $518,539 ($3,662/month × 12 months × 11.8).

So, with $25,000 in savings with modest home equity, you're indeed far behind.

It probably makes sense to consider deferring retirement until age seventy if you're in good health. That will help in three ways. First, the 25 percent increase in Social Security payments reduces the required lump sum by about $58,000. Second, you have five years longer to save (twenty total, not fifteen), and third, you may only need to cover fifteen years of retirement. That translates, with a 9.7 factor for fifteen years (see Accumulation Annuity Table on page 21), to a new lump sum requirement of $378,241 ($5,312 − S.S. of $2,062 = $3,249/month net need × 12 × 9.7). Now using accumulation annuity math with a factor of 36.8 for twenty years at 6 percent, you get an annual required savings of $10,278. The implied 12 percent of income saved ($10,278/$85,000) shouldn't be too difficult, especially with employer match, tax benefits, and catch-up contribution provisions.

Question 130: **Scenario: I am forty and really want to retire early. Can I? How? My assets are income $80,000, home $250,000, mortgage $175,000 at 7.5 percent, current savings $40,000, and retirement savings $60,000.**

The first step is to decide how early to retire. Retirement before fifty-five really puts a burden on savings, for you need to plan at least thirty years of retirement and at least seven years without Social Security. You also need to consider health care and whether you can retire early from a job with some health benefits.

Without repeating the detailed analysis of Question 129 (it is more detailed because of the Social Security issue), it's best to think in terms of a three-part strategy. First, plan to pay off the home before you retire. That implies a 15-year mortgage or shorter. Next, you should practice living cheap for two reasons: first, it will help later to survive on something less than the rule of thumb of 70 to 80 percent of current income, and second, because it allows some power savings during the next fifteen years. Finally, those power savings should be invested aggressively with the notion that, if successful, you can indeed retire early; if unfortunately you are less successful, you still have some time to build the nest egg. The bottom line is pay off the mortgage, learn to live frugally, and stretch your investments a bit, and you have a shot at it.

Chapter 10

ABOUT INVESTING

How do you achieve life goals such as retirement, college, a new television, or a bigger house? By accumulating wealth. How do you accumulate wealth? Surely it starts with adequate savings. But it is difficult to achieve financial independence on savings alone. To build a substantial nest egg, those savings have to work, too. That "work" is investing—the deployment of capital to achieve a return. The nature of that work is unique, for it can feed on itself through the effects of compounding. At the end of the day, investing is a powerful tool to achieve the wealth to which most people aspire.

The chief goals of investing are asset protection and asset growth. This chapter explores investing basics and the many different paths to achieving investing objectives.

Question 131: **Why is investing so important in personal finance?**

The general model for building wealth in personal finance can be summarized in the phrase "make it, keep it, grow it." Investing is the *grow it* part.

In the long term, the *income replacement model* suggests that the power to earn through work declines over time, especially into retirement, and income needs are supplied increasingly by returns on assets. So the amount of income you have and, ultimately, your lifestyle depend on the amount of assets you can accumulate—your golden goose. It is the returns on these assets—the eggs—that produce income. Investing is an important way to get ahead during working years and to *stay* ahead during retirement.

Question 132: **I have my savings in a bank. Is this investing?**

Technically, "yes." Your money is set aside, and it is earning a return. But that return may be 1 to 2 percent depending on the type of account. With inflation running approximately 3 percent, that money is actually losing purchasing power. If it is being saved for college, where costs are escalating nearly 6 percent annually, these savings are losing ground. On the other hand, as these savings are insured, the investment is very safe. You have achieved protection, but not growth.

Good investing means deploying your capital to grow faster than inflation. It involves taking calculated risks to achieve these returns, requiring a degree of careful management either by you or a financial professional. Long-term wealth building requires beating inflation and riding the compounding train to get the most out of that capital.

Question 133: **Please give a summary of the major investment types I need to be familiar with.**

The investing world is wide; here is a brief summary.

> *Stocks* represent investments in businesses, that is, the deployment of capital to share in the returns of the business. "Sharing" can be through receipt of actual cash payments—*dividends*—or by sharing in the growth of the company as valued by the stock market. The stock market values companies through the collective voice of others buying and selling shares in the company.

Bonds also represent investments in a business—or government or public agency—with a promise of a specific return in a specific time. Corporate bond investors trade away participation in business success for this promise.

Mutual funds are investment companies established to buy and manage a "basket" of stocks and/or bonds on your behalf. *Index funds* are a special type of fund set up to track specific stock indexes such as the S&P 500, requiring relatively less (and less expensive) professional management.

Real estate investments can be direct, that is, in specific properties, or indirect, through funds designed to purchase real property assets.

Commodities are raw materials, agricultural products, or key business inputs like gold, oil, wheat, soybeans, or foreign currencies. You can invest directly by buying gold or currencies, but it is more practical to buy and sell *futures* contracts for future delivery of these materials or to buy stock in producing companies.

Question 134: **What is the long-term track record for the major types of investments?**

Over the long term, stocks have performed the best for the active management of resources by a corporate entity, and participation in the growth in the economy has prevailed. During the past seventy-five years, stocks have achieved average annual returns of about 11 percent but with significant year-to-year variation, especially in recent years. In that period, stocks achieved negative returns in about twenty-one of those years. That volatility subsides over time; in fact, in no fifteen-year period since the 1920s have stocks produced a negative return. Corporate bonds have achieved returns of about 6 percent per year with less than half the volatility of stocks, and government bonds have achieved about 5 percent with still less volatility. Real estate has performed about in line with stocks with less variability in overall annual performance. Because direct real estate purchases can be leveraged with debt (mortgages), returns for many have been higher, but there are also management costs and time.

Question 135: **Are there good rules about how to allocate my investments among different types?**

Age and risk tolerance are the two main factors governing allocation among different types of investments. As you get older, it becomes more important to preserve—rather than grow—the nest egg; so investments should shift toward the relatively less volatile bonds, cash, and possibly income-producing real estate. Financial planners use a standard rule limiting "growth" (riskier) investments to a figure equal to 100 minus your age. That is, if you are thirty-five, then 65 percent of your assets should be invested aggressively; that figure drops to 40 percent at age sixty.

Risk tolerance is more difficult to quantify, although many financial advisors attempt to do so through surveys and questionnaires. Some people prefer riskier investments to achieve the return; others just can't sleep at night. Riskier investments require closer tracking and more time spent. Your own risk profile is important, and if you can't take the idea of losing 20 percent in a year, then stay away from individual stocks and aggressive small-company growth funds that can lose this amount.

Question 136: **How actively involved can/should I be in managing my investments?**

This question has really come into the spotlight in recent years as it has become more apparent that many financial professionals—securities analysts, brokers, mutual fund managers—have acted more on their own behalf than for their clients. The answer really depends on how much time you prefer and have to spend managing your investments. Even the most sophisticated investors delegate the management of some portion of their investments—maybe a retirement or college fund—to professionals. The best advice is to learn as much as possible about investing and delegate wisely. Even if you bring in professionals, you need to follow what they're doing. Remember it's your money.

Question 137: **As an investor, it is obvious that I need to stay informed. What are the best basic information sources?**

Driven in part by technology, business change is accelerating relentlessly, and the financial markets that follow it have become more volatile. Unless you have a financial advisor whom you trust wholeheartedly, you need to keep pace, at least by reading the newspaper. More involved investors use financial newspapers (*The Wall Street Journal, Investor's Business Daily*) to stay on top of business and marketplace trends. Technology, while accelerating change, also provides a vast set of tools to keep track. Yahoo!Finance (*finance. yahoo.com*) and other financial portals do an excellent job of bringing business, market, and financial planning tools together.

Question 138: **I am a beginning investor. Should I use a full-service broker?**

Brokerage houses provide a wide range of services, from simple execution of trades to varying degrees of "value-add" in the form of financial advice and research services. *Full-service brokers* such as Merrill Lynch and Edward Jones offer a designated account manager for your account, a staff of research analysts, proprietary investment reports and stock ratings, and other investing resources. But you pay; commissions can be ten times that for a *discount broker*. Discount brokers mainly operate through the Internet and telephone agent trading, with an assortment of investing resources available. Most offer little in the way of proprietary information and individual coaching, but you can buy and sell stocks for as little as $10 per trade. The industry is moving to a middle ground where companies like Charles Schwab offer assorted service options from straight Internet trading to face-to-face advisory services. Some of these extra offerings are available for free if you have enough in your account.

To answer the question, full-service brokers make sense if you plan to buy individual stocks, have little time or interest in the markets, and want personalized advice. Most brokers offer financial advice beyond investments but be careful as they may not be fully trained or qualified to offer such advice. For more "do-it-yourself" oriented individuals, discount brokerage products are usually enough. If you plan to invest strictly in mutual funds, you don't need a broker at all; you can invest directly with the fund company.

Question 139: **How do I choose a discount broker?**

Television and newspaper advertising is packed with ads for different brokerage services—discounters like E-Trade, Ameritrade, and Waterhouse Securities and an assortment of full-service brokers. Discount brokers compete by offering free trades, shaving a few cents from commissions, two-second execution promises, and availability of basic research materials such as Standard & Poor's stock reports. In reality there is little real difference, and the choice mostly comes down to customer service and the suitability of Web sites to your taste. Can you get good phone support? Can you get stock quotes and make trades by phone when away from your normal workplace? Does their Web site meet your expectations for ease of use? A good investment idea should be a good idea ten seconds from now; so don't worry about execution speed. Remember, a good investing strategy with a bad broker beats a bad investing strategy with a good broker.

Question 140: **What is the case for investing in individual stocks?**

When you invest in stocks, you participate in the growth of the U.S. economy. If you choose the right companies, they will outpace the economy. In the long run, owning corporate equities is the most proven way to beat inflation. By buying stock, you become an owner, employing professionals to generate superior cash returns by being the best in their business.

However, as has been so vividly demonstrated in recent years, it's hard to know whether those professionals are really working for you (just think of Enron, WorldCom, etc.) It can be quite difficult to ferret out the best companies in good businesses since the landscape changes constantly (for example, Eastman Kodak, Lucent Technologies). The bottom line: investing in individual companies brings risk and a lot of work on your part to sort out these issues. The mantra "risk brings reward" applies and vice versa.

Question 141: **What is the case for bond investing?**

With bonds, you lend money to a company to get a predetermined fixed and generally safe return on your investment. Bonds represent safety and predictability; however, in most market conditions, returns are modest and only slightly—2 to 3 percent—ahead of inflation. The bond investing world is somewhat mysterious and oriented to institutional and professional investors. Individual bond characteristics and credit risk information are hard to get and still harder to interpret, and mistakes can be very costly. When buying and selling individual bonds, you should probably do so through a financial professional, which adds to the cost. Bond-oriented mutual funds are an alternative, but costs further dilute returns. Some form of bond or fixed income investment is probably a good idea to anchor a portfolio to insulate it from stock market cycles. But there are alternatives such as dividend-paying stocks and paying off your mortgage.

Question 142: **What is the case for mutual fund investing?**

Mutual funds have been the most popular way for typical U.S. households to invest over the last forty years. With a mutual fund, you essentially employ a professional manager and research resources of an investment company (Putnam, T. Rowe Price, Fidelity, etc.) to invest for you. Investors seeking less involvement and long-term performance find this attractive. Mutual funds provide diversification that individuals can't achieve and are generally safer than pursuing individual investments. Mutual funds have consumerized their products with friendly marketing and customer service.

There are downsides to fund investing. The first is *cost*. Professional management and marketing expenses are passed on to fundholders, adding up to 2 percent or more of a fund's value annually. Costs can seriously dilute performance. As a result, some 70 to 90 percent (depending on which study you read) of funds underperform the market as a whole.

Second, and called more into question recently, is the quality and integrity of fund *management*. Are they really working for you? The third is fund *transparency*—it is hard to know how the fund is invested today and what management is really doing. Finally, by *overtrading*, some funds create tax surprises and tend to further underperform in the long term. Still, funds can offer good value to individual investors and can accomplish what many can't or don't want to do themselves. Finding alternative funds with lower fees can help. Index funds that track major stock market indices, reducing management activity, and the recently arrived *Exchange Traded Funds* (ETFs) are worth a look—see Question 181.

Question 143: **What is the case for real estate investing?**

Real estate has been a hot investment, particularly in the flat 2000–04 equity market period. The recent boom has been fueled by low interest rates, and since most real estate is bought with large loans (mortgages), that has made higher prices affordable. An influx of immigrants has fueled demand particularly in coastal areas. Real estate is attractive because it is tangible, and as investors like to say, "they ain't making any more of it." Appreciation helps in resale and to attract higher rents—cash flow—on investment property during a long ownership period. Real estate has proven to be a good hedge—defense—against inflation. Further, real estate is the only investment where you can improve value through your own hard work and ingenuity.

There are downsides. Appreciation is by no means a sure thing; real estate is extremely sensitive to interest rates and location. People tend to underestimate the time and cost to maintain properties.

Question 144: **What is the case for commodity investing?**

Commodities are the raw materials and inputs to business and consumption. Logically, anything where demand is growing and supply is constant makes sense to own as an investment. Such has been experienced with the recent "China effect" on industrial inputs, especially oil. Commodities, especially those with more constrained supply, make sense as a hedge against inflation and as a "globalization" play.

However, investing in commodities is very difficult. There are many market forces at play, most beyond the knowledge and comprehension of the individual investor. "Constrained supply" tends to become less constrained as prices rise; there are few "sure thing" investments. Commodities like gold, owned directly, produce no cash returns and may in fact cost money to own (storage costs, etc). Most commodity investors use futures contracts, a very market-sensitive and time-specific investment form. That is, you must be right about both *what* happens and *when* it happens. Commodity investments require more time and experience than most investors have available. Investing in commodity-oriented businesses such as metal, timber, gold, or oil producers can be a good substitute, but company performance in that sector comes into play.

Question 145: **What is NASDAQ, and how is it different from the NYSE?**

NASDAQ and NYSE (New York Stock Exchange) are the two biggest *stock markets,* that is, venues where individuals and dealers come together to buy and sell stocks. NASDAQ stands for National Association of Securities Dealers Automated Quotations and is essentially a computerized bulletin board where dealers and some individuals can post quotes. Dealers, known as *marketmakers,* make markets for specific securities and must post quotations for a *bid*— what they would pay you for a stock, and an *ask,* the price at which they would sell you the stock. Generally, your "buy" order is filled by the marketmaker with sufficient shares available at the lowest quoted price on the electronic board. Advanced Level II screens make it possible to see quotes for all dealers in the market.

Unlike NASDAQ, which is analogous to the free market capitalism found in any open market, the NYSE is set up as an auction market, where all sales are handled by an auctioneer known as a *specialist*. The specialist matches buy and sell orders and quotes the best bid and offer price for orders in hand or for purchases and sales from their own inventory.

Until recently, NYSE has been the elite marketplace for more established companies, while NASDAQ has flourished for younger growth-oriented companies. That is changing as the NYSE specialist system is questioned for fairness and as Internet technology brings NASDAQ transparency to more people. For most investors, whether a stock is NYSE listed or NASDAQ makes little difference.

Question 146: **How should I decide whether to invest in mutual funds or individual stocks?**

Basically, individual stock investing requires two essential ingredients: money and time. *Money* means having sufficient funds to buy enough different stocks to achieve some safety through diversification and large enough quantities of those stocks to avoid excessive transaction costs. Markets set *round lot* purchase quantities of 100 shares or more; anything less is known as an *odd lot* and will cost somewhat more to buy and sell. So you need enough funds to buy round lot quantities in a few—at least three or four—companies.

More than money, individual stock investing requires *time*, that is, time to understand the business in which you are investing. That means understanding the marketplace in which the company sells its product and the company's financial performance. Big companies are complex, and understanding these factors is no small task. It takes time and some business and financial knowledge.

For those just starting out or those who prefer to leave the management to someone else, mutual funds or professional advisors may be a better bet.

Question 147: **Most media stock market reports highlight the Dow Jones Industrial Average. Is it still a good indicator of market performance?**

The "Dow" has been around since about the turn of the last century and is still the simple answer to the question: "What did the market do today?" The Dow Jones Industrial Average (DJIA) is comprised of thirty *blue chip,* or top-quality, stocks. Not too long ago, these were truly old-line industrial companies like U.S. Steel, General Motors, Caterpillar, and Goodyear Tire & Rubber. While some old names remain, recent changes have moved the group away from heavy manufacturing into such service and technology names as Wal-Mart, Microsoft, Intel, and Johnson & Johnson. So the index today reflects a broader, more service-oriented economy.

The Dow is only thirty companies, and it tends to be the "bluest" of the blue chips. So many market followers prefer the broader Standard & Poor's 500 Stock Index (S&P 500). While this index became overweighted with technology names during the late 1990s boom, today's company mix is more aligned to the overall economy and market. From its 2000 peak to mid-2004, the S&P 500 declined 33 percent, while the DJIA declined about 16 percent. Which is a better indicator? You make the call.

Question 148: **What is a stock really worth?**

This is a tough question, and the theoretical and practical answers are both important for the average investor. The theoretical value of a stock is the present value of all future cash returns from the stock. *Present value* means that dollars in hand today are worth more than dollars received in the future. So a stock with "predictable" cash returns occurring "sooner" is worth more. *Future cash returns* are normally from earnings and dividends but can be from the eventual sale of all or part of the company. The trick is deciding whether potential future returns and uncertainty surrounding those returns are worth today's price.

The practical answer: a stock is worth whatever the collective judgment of market participants say it's worth, through actual purchases and sales of the stock. The market price reflects this collective wisdom, which, at the end of the day reflects the collective assessment of future cash returns—in normal times, anyway. Distorted perceptions or total ignorance of future cash returns causes market value to get away from real value, which is what happened in the late 1990s.

Question 149: **Please compare and contrast growth and value investing.**

Growth investors seek growing companies in growing industries, usually expecting 5 percent or more growth in revenues (and earnings) each year. Growth investments are usually found in growth industries, such as high tech or biotech. They may also be found in traditional industries, where a new approach or change in trends or tastes creates growth through market share gains (e.g., Starbucks in the restaurant/refreshment industry). Growth investors are willing to pay more for stocks than worth based on today's returns (in fact, many lose money) but are betting on strong future returns.

Value investors look for value in hand today—strong assets, low debt, strong earnings and cash flows, dividends, and appreciably strong market positions in their industry. They are especially attracted to situations where these factors are underestimated by the market, that is, where the stock sells at a discount to real value. Value investors look at a stock as a business, buying the stock as though they were buying the business for themselves, with all the diligence that implies. Value investors minimize risk with tangible value; that value protects them from major downside swings. They also look for competitive barriers, such as a strong brand, that build protective "moats" around the business.

Recently the growth and value approaches have converged. Indeed, value investors too want to see growth potential in the businesses they buy, and they seek situations where that growth potential is undervalued in the market. "Growth At a Reasonable Price," or "(GARP)," is their investing mantra. Within this idea, even companies like Starbucks, with a strong brand and a 20 to 25 percent annual growth rate, can be considered a value stock.

Question 150: I hear a lot about dollar-cost averaging. Is this just a buzzword, or is it something to know more about?

Dollar-cost averaging is one of the few buzzword investing clichés commonly heard on AM radio financial shows that has real and enduring merit. Dollar-cost averaging is investing a relatively fixed amount in a mutual fund (or individual stock or stock portfolio) over time. The wisdom: with a constant investment, you buy relatively more shares during downturns and relatively fewer shares during periods of strength. Thus, it serves to lower your average entry price into the investment, and it further serves as a regular savings vehicle. Of course, it doesn't guarantee success—the investment itself must be right, too, but you will enjoy improved performance even with a modestly performing investment.

Question 151: What is a portfolio, and how do I build one?

A *portfolio* is a collection of individual stocks, mutual funds, bonds, and other investments balanced to achieve an investor's objectives while minimizing risk. A portfolio reduces risk by avoiding over-concentration—an "all-eggs-in-one-basket" approach—in a single investment. Overconcentration is tempting to new investors seeking to "hit a home run" with a novel investing idea or to investors with too little money to invest to achieve diversification.

Typically, good portfolios first allocate assets between *asset classes*—usually stocks, bonds, real estate, and cash. The allocation percentage depends on an investor's age, tolerance for risk, and near-term needs, and it is a favorite topic of most financial advisors. Within each asset class, the portfolio has a diversified mix of stocks, bonds, and funds.

Typically, a diversified stock or bond portfolio holds five to ten companies, while a mutual fund portfolio might hold three to seven funds (fewer because of the diversification implied in funds). Funds are usually substituted when an investor has insufficient resources or knowledge to diversify with individual investments. While the risk of underdiversification is overexposure to the fortunes of a single business, there is also a risk of *overdiversification*—that is, spreading among too many investments—and achieving at best market returns while incurring excessive costs. The bottom line: get help when you need it.

Question 152: **How do I select a stock?**

This is the $64,000 question of investing—stock investing, anyway. Among the thousands of publicly traded issues to select from, how do you go about it?

The answer could fill an entire book. We'll choose the value investor's approach. Look at the stock as a share in a business and determine if the business is congruent to your investing objectives.

Part of the answer lies in your investing objective. Are you looking for relatively certain cash returns relatively soon, as would be indicated by a high dividend? If so, your choices would likely include utilities and other staid investments with little growth, strong cash flow, and little risk. If, like most stock investors, you're looking for a balance of short-term and long-term return potential, the *business value model* comes into play.

Value investors look for situations where a company has achieved strong and growing *marketplace position*, through brand excellence, operational excellence, proprietary technology, or some other superlative set of attributes or skills. Next, they look for evidence that such marketplace excellence has translated into *financial success*—strong and growing profits, profit margins, cash flow, and return on deployed assets and stockholder's equity. Such a determination is hardly simple. This author's book *Value Investing for Dummies* (Wiley, 2002) goes deeper. Finally, once the business prospects are determined to be above average, the investor looks for a *good price*—that is, a share price—at which to buy. It takes detailed research to make the selection. For this answer, it's the thought process that's important.

Question 153: **How do I tell if a business (stock) is improving or has declining prospects?**

This is another fundamental question for individual stock investors. Like investing itself, assessing future prospects usually mixes analysis and common sense. The common sense part is sort of an ear-to-the-ground exercise. Is the company improving its products or services? Does the marketplace accept the product? What do people say about the product on the street and in the press? Do the company and its products have a positive or negative image? Is the product "in," or is it a leftover of some gradually disappearing past? Contrast the fortunes of Eastman Kodak, General Motors, and Hewlett-Packard with those of Starbucks, Toyota, and Dell. One must be careful not to rely too much on personal opinion and not to get caught up in fads.

The analytical answer involves reviewing certain key financials. Are profits improving? How about profit margins? Are revenues increasing faster than costs? How about productivity—the revenues and profits delivered per dollar invested, per store owned, per employee? The list of indicators is long, but in the end, they all indicate the sort of excellence—or lack thereof—discerned by the common-sense analysis.

Question 154: **How do I tell if a stock is overvalued?**

There is no surefire way to tell if a stock is overvalued, for many stocks that appear expensive relative to current performance have strong and often legitimate growth prospects built into their prices.

Most investors grade stocks by their *P/E* (price-to-earnings ratio), computed by dividing the stock price by the most recent twelve months' reported earnings. Recent historic average marketwide P/Es tend to range from about 16 to 23. *Earnings yield,* the inverse of P/E, is a way to make sense of the figure. A P/E of 20 implies an earnings yield of 5 percent (1/20), a yardstick to compare to alternative investments.

Adding more information is the *PEG* (Price/Earnings/Growth ratio), relating P/E to the growth rate. So a stock with a P/E of 20 and a 20 percent growth rate has a PEG of 1, an attractive level. But earnings are subject to many onetime factors, manipulations, and special, noncash accounting events like depreciation. As a result, many investors are attracted to more pure measures such as price-to-cash-flow, but that may fail to properly judge capital investments.

In general, stocks appear overvalued if they have no significant earnings prospects or if the P/E is greater than 25 (and especially if the PEG is greater than 3). Although these ratios are good indicators, real answers lie deeper in the fundamentals of marketplace and financial performance, where market share and profit margins can be telling.

Question 155: **What is meant by market cap, and why is it important?**

Market cap, or market capitalization, is the number of shares of a company outstanding multiplied by the share price. So a company with 100 million shares outstanding at a price of $20 has a market cap of $2 billion. Why is this important? First, for those investing in a stock as a business, market cap gives a big-picture view of business value. Is Starbucks worth $18 billion as a company? Is Cisco worth $140 billion? Was Cisco worth $500 billion during the bubble? You be the judge.

Market cap is also used to segment companies for investing through mutual funds. Many mutual funds target "large cap" (> $5 billion), "mid cap" ($1 billion to $5 billion), or "small cap" (< $1 billion) companies. As an investor in these funds, you'll know the kinds of companies in which they invest.

Question 156: **I have it now. When do I sell it?**

This may be the hardest question in investing. Selling is hard to do. Many marry their investments, hoping that things go better someday even if things are rotten today. Likewise, some dump the investment at the first sign of trouble. What's the right answer?

There is, of course, no right answer, for there is no such thing as perfect business judgment. The best answers are (1) sell when an investment meets your investing objective (which of course implies that you set an investing objective in the first place) and (2) sell when there is something else better to buy. Those who use both of these principles will usually come out ahead.

Question 157: **Recent market volatility scares me. What should I do about it?**

Indeed, you have reason for concern. The increasing pace of global business and economic change has caused markets to become more volatile. The S&P 500 Stock Index has closed up or down more than 10 percent in nine of the last ten years, compared to only four times in the prior ten years. The NASDAQ Composite Index has been still more volatile. What can you do?

- *Expect it.* Markets will rise and fall; don't agonize over each 100-point drop in the Dow Industrials.
- *Prepare for it.* Don't overload with stocks too sensitive to economic and market swings.
- *Take advantage of it.* The more active investor uses downturns to buy value investments at a lower price. Consider downturns an opportunity, not just a problem.

Question 158: **How do I defend my portfolio from loss?**

You can't protect against everything, for if you did you would also destroy the potential for future gains. But there are a few ways to protect against the worst.

- *Play defense.* Allocate portions of your portfolio to investments relatively immune to economic change, so-called *defensive* stocks like consumer nondurables, food, and defense contractors. Bad times cause relatively little disruption as people tend to buy even when the economic outlook is poor. Global instability may even help defense contractors.
- *Diversify.* While it may not help with global economic and market declines, diversifying your investments helps defend against individual company blowups.
- *Buy "insurance."* You can buy investment insurance in the form of *put options* (puts), giving you the right to sell shares at a certain price. You can also buy "puts" on market indexes like the S&P 500. Defensive-minded investors should learn about these tools.

Question 159: **Are stock splits a good thing?**

In theory, "no"; in practice, "sometimes." With a stock split, a company simply expands the number of shares outstanding according to the ratio of the split: a company with 100 million shares selling at $40 per share goes to 200 million shares at $20 per share with a 2-for-1 split. Have you gained anything? No. If you had 100 shares at $40 per share and now have 200 shares at $20 per share, you have the same investment in the company.

However, stock splits are seen as a signal that management expects improving business prospects and growth in the share price. So there may be a positive influence on market perception. But as markets since 2000 have become more driven by value than perception, this effect has subsided in recent years, and splits are largely a nonevent.

Question 160: **I am looking at two companies, one pays a dividend, and the other doesn't. Which is the better investment?**

With recent tax changes favoring dividends, the debate on this subject has come back into the spotlight. Dividends are cash returns, usually paid out of earnings, to shareholders as a return on their invested capital. Dividends are strictly a management decision, not a legal requirement. Companies that don't pay a dividend simply reinvest earnings into the business.

Some think dividends are a bad sign because companies are admitting they don't have anything better to do with the capital. That is, there are no available projects or businesses that would produce a favorable return, and so they may as well distribute the funds to stockholders. Others hold that management teams concerned about shareholder interests are willing to pay shareholders for their investments. Recognizing shareholders and meeting business needs simultaneously is a sign of good management.

Today's prudent investor is likely to view dividends as a good sign and enjoy the favorable tax treatment as well. The only exception would be in a rapidly growing business with large capital requirements (thus requiring reinvestment), but such cases need to be justified. No reinvesting would-be dividends in fancy corporate jets!

Question 161: **What are the pros and cons of buying stocks on margin?**

Margin refers to funds borrowed from your broker to buy stocks. Investors can set up a *margin account* relatively easily and borrow up to 50 percent of the amount of a new stock purchase. Margin provides additional *leverage,* that is, more of an asset can be owned producing potentially higher returns on the invested capital. Margin interest rates are competitive and may be income tax deductible against earnings from the investment.

On the flip side, margin is debt, like any other debt. The leverage works in reverse if investments decline. That is, the asset may go away, but the debt doesn't. In fact, if your equity declines below 35 percent of your investment portfolio, you will get a call (a *margin call*) from your broker for more funds. On the whole, margin is mainly for careful use by experienced investors.

Question 162: **I hear recent tax changes have favored investors. How?**

Starting in 2003, the maximum federal income tax rate for both long-term capital gains and qualified dividends is 15 percent. Prior to this change, dividends were taxed as ordinary income, subject to tax rates up to 35 percent. Long-term capital gains—that is, for assets held more than one year—were taxed at a maximum rate of 20 percent, and short-term gains were taxed as ordinary income. This change makes certain kinds of investments, particularly dividend-paying stocks, much more attractive.

Question 163: **My uncle says he makes a lot of money selling stocks short. Can you comment on this strategy?**

Short sellers make money by borrowing shares from their brokers and selling them, hoping to buy them back later at a lower price. Obviously, short sellers hope for market drops and declines in the fortunes of the companies they "short."

When you sell short, you risk the possibility that the stock could go up indefinitely. This is the primary risk of short selling. Also, because of a Depression-era rule, short sales must occur on an *uptick,* that is, an improvement from the most recent price, making it harder to jump on the bandwagon of a stock already going down. You must see something others don't. Short sellers must actively manage the progress of their investments, for long-term exposure to short positions is risky. Finally, borrowing shares can be costly; you have to pay margin interest rates and for any dividends lost by the original owner during the borrowing period.

With that said, many have done well by short selling, especially in recent years. Short selling is a good way to play both sides of the market for investors inclined toward short-term opportunities.

Question 164: **Give a summary of the different kinds of bonds and how they would be used in different portfolios.**

Bonds can be classified as follows:

> *Government and corporate*—Government bonds include federal, state, and local governments and a variety of quasigovernmental agencies such as transit districts. Government bonds are relatively safe and usually at least partially tax-exempt but pay lower returns as a result. Corporate bonds generally pay more but are taxable and more risky.

> *Taxable and tax-exempt*—Many government or agency bonds are exempt from some taxes. Municipal bonds, for instance, are federal tax exempt. U.S. Treasury securities are usually exempt from local and state taxes and federal-taxable only on a deferred (at maturity) basis. Tax-exempt bonds are attractive to high-income investors.

> *Investment grade and "junk" bonds*—Investment grade bonds have been judged by credit agencies such as Standard & Poor's and Moody's to be solid credit risks; that is, investors are most likely to get their capital repaid. "Junk" bonds entail more

credit risk but pay higher rates, sometimes several percentage points higher.

Short-term and long-term bonds—Short-term bonds are due (that is, principal is repaid) usually in five years or less, while long-term bonds can be ten, fifteen, thirty, or even forty years out. Long-term bonds lock in an interest rate, but if this rate is exceeded by current market conditions, it will lose value. Short-term bonds are better for those seeking to preserve value but usually pay lower interest rates.

Question 165: My friend tells me that I should invest in bonds because they are risk free. Is this right?

While bonds may bring less risk than most stocks, bond investing is hardly risk free. Bonds come with a promise that known amounts of money will be paid back on specific dates, thus reducing risk. Nevertheless, there is some risk that the company or agency won't be able to repay, known as *credit risk*. Only the U.S. Treasury is generally assumed to have zero credit risk. Choosing high-grade companies and agencies reduces credit risks.

Next is *interest rate risk*. If you buy a bond paying 5 percent and prevailing interest rates rise to 9 percent, what happens to the value of your bond? Because a bond investor today can buy a 9 percent bond, your 5 percent bond is worth less to them. So the market price of your bond declines accordingly, in fact, enough to make your bond pay 9 percent to the new investor.

Finally, there is *inflation risk*. Rising inflation means that principal paid back to you later has less purchasing power. The longer the time to maturity, the greater the inflation and interest rate risk. More can happen during longer time periods, so investors buy shorter-term maturities, paying lower returns, to avoid these risks.

Question 166: How do I tell if a bond is "junk"?

The quick answer: don't try to tell on your own! Credit risk analysis is very complex and best left to the major credit agencies such as

Standard & Poor's, Moody's, and Fitch's. Standard & Poor's assigns grades of "BBB" and higher (BBB, A, AA, AAA) to investment-grade bonds; everything "BB" and lower is junk. For Moody's, investment grade is "Baa" and higher. Note that there are many shades of junk—D, C, CC, CCC, B, and BB on the S&P scale; so there are many choices of risk/return profiles you can choose. The trick of junk bond investing is to make sure the additional return is worth the risk taken and to diversify heavily—for most investors this means investing through funds.

Question 167: How can I learn more about specific bond investments?

Unfortunately, the bond-investing world is fairly opaque and largely oriented to institutional and fund investors. There are few easy sources of information available about individual bonds. Internet financial portals such as Yahoo!Finance provide some very basic bond information but not really enough quality or quantity to choose and evaluate bonds investments. Investing in bonds—particularly individual bonds as opposed to bond funds—will likely have to work through a broker or financial professional.

Question 168: Which are better—taxable bonds or tax-exempt bonds? When and why?

Tax-exempt bonds are primarily attractive to higher income investors. While a good quality corporate bond may pay 5 or 6 percent, a comparable municipal bond might pay 4 or 5 percent. Which is the better choice? For investors in a 30-percent combined tax bracket, a 5 percent municipal yield is roughly equivalent to a 7-plus percent corporate yield. Some investors are in a higher tax bracket. The bottom line: investors need to pencil it out for themselves, but municipal bonds have been attractive recently.

Question 169: Give me a crash course on U.S. Treasury bonds.

U.S. Treasury credit instruments are offered in many varieties, some more and some less oriented to individual consumer investors:

Treasury bills, notes, and *bonds* can be purchased directly or in secondary markets in denominations of $1,000 or more. Bills mature in one year or less, notes mature in one to ten years, and bonds, reflecting a recent change, also mature in ten years (formerly thirty years). Interest rates typically increase with time to maturity, while prices will fluctuate more.

Treasury Inflation Protection Securities (TIPS) are a new, specialized type of note or bond paying nominal interest plus an amount indexed to the current level of inflation. Investors looking to eliminate inflation risk (see Question 165) are attracted to these bonds with good reason; they are a good cornerstone investment.

Savings bonds are the consumer-friendly Treasury product, bought and sold in increments as low as $25 from the Treasury or through local banks. Savings bonds are bought at a discount—that is, you pay a reduced amount and redeem at face value. Some savings bond interest can be tax-free if used for education.

Treasury bond investors should visit the Treasury Direct Web site *(www.treasurydirect.gov)* to learn more and buy directly.

Question 170: **I'm concerned about how rising interest rates might affect my portfolio. What should I do?**

Rising interest rates make the bonds you own less attractive to investors in the market so the value will decline, particularly if your bonds have a long time before reaching maturity. There are two approaches to reduce this risk. First, you can shift to shorter maturities, sacrificing some return. Second, you can "ladder" your portfolio, spreading bonds across many maturities—some maturing this year, some maturing next year, some maturing five years out, and so forth. Unfortunately, this process is hard to achieve with small portfolios. Most bond funds employ this strategy but watch out for high fees and costs.

Question 171: **I like the idea of investing in income-producing securities, but I'm not sure bonds are for me. What are some alternatives?**

Bond investing is thought by many to be boring and mysterious and expensive as well. Commissions and fees can eat up potential return, and credit, interest rate, and inflation risks are hard to eliminate.

Paying off a mortgage, for most, is an intriguing alternative. It isn't investing in the traditional sense, but it can be largely equivalent to buying a bond at your mortgage interest rate. The interest saved is your return, and tax-wise it is largely a wash (you lose the mortgage interest deduction but don't pay taxes on the bond interest). If you can't afford to pay off the whole mortgage, benefits aren't realized immediately but accrue as future interest savings. But most bond-related risks go away. Liquidity fears—that is, fear that cash will be tied up—go away with today's easy availability of home equity credit lines.

Other alternatives include preferred stocks and certificates of deposit (CDs). Preferred stocks are like a bond but with no definite maturity and more credit risk. Like bonds, they are hard for consumer investors to evaluate. CDs are conveniently available at local financial institutions but pay low returns. Ordinary dividend-paying common stocks, especially with today's tax rules, have become more attractive but bring risks of their own.

Question 172: **What are mutual funds?**

Mutual funds are investment companies—companies formed for the specific purpose of investing under the Investment Act of 1940. Investment companies must pass through at least 90 percent of earnings to investors and must have several investment holdings. In return, investment company earnings aren't taxed. Mutual fund investment companies invest in a changeable mix of securities, and they may be actively managed or follow an index. *Unit investment trusts* have a fixed set of investments at the beginning—often something besides securities—and usually terminate at some point. Real estate investment trusts are an example. Finally, Exchange Traded Funds are an emerging hybrid, with some characteristics of mutual funds and some characteristics of unit investment trusts.

Numbering over 9,200 today, conventional mutual funds have brought investing to the consumer. They offer a value proposition of professional management, consumer-friendly information, access, and customer service all delivered for a price.

Question 173: Can you elaborate on the costs of mutual fund investing?

Many mutual funds have come under fire recently for the size and complexity of their "price tag" to their investors. Funds routinely charge management fees for choosing and managing holdings, ranging from 0.10 percent to 1.5 percent or more of a fund's value. This doesn't sound like much until you add up totals, which can approach $1 billion for the largest funds, considering only a minority of funds outperforms the market. Further, funds charge *12-b-1 fees*, passing through marketing and distribution costs up to 0.75 percent (plus 0.25 percent for a service fee). It covers customer service costs and the commissions paid broker salespeople to acquire new investors. So you pay your fund to bring other investors on board. Finally, *load funds* charge investors a direct commission in addition to these other fees, amounting to as much as 5 percent and effectively locking an investor in for fear of forfeiting the commission. *No-load funds* pull these costs from investment value. Aside from loads, fees of 1 to 3 percent and sometimes more can eat a big chunk of today's more conservative 6 to 8 percent annual investment returns. Meanwhile, index and other inactively managed funds may charge half a percent or less. Fund investors should check the *expense ratio*—a summary of all fees—and decide whether they're getting value for their money.

Question 174: How should most investors use mutual funds?

Mutual funds are useful for those with limited resources and limited time to manage their own investments. Investors with limited assets can still participate in the larger market. Investors lacking time or who just don't want to manage investments can leave the management to someone else. In short, funds offer ease of entry, expertise, convenience, and diversification.

Through professionally managed and balanced holdings, mutual funds help investors diversify by definition. Funds provide a path to invest in challenging sectors like international stocks and biotech, where expertise is beyond the average investor's reach. Finally, funds provide the primary vehicle for investing in many college savings plans (like so-called 529 plans) and are usually an effective way to invest retirement assets for the long term. Most investors are well served to have a mix of funds and individual investments, the mix determined by personal preference and interest in investing.

Question 175: **In general, how many mutual funds should I own?**

The short answer: more than one but not too many. It usually makes no sense to own more than one fund in the same category—for example, two large cap U.S. stock funds. Why? Because their investments will overlap. If you own too many funds, the resulting overdiversification costs a lot of money for a set of investments unlikely to deviate much from overall market performance. You're better off to buy a low-cost index fund and walk away. A portfolio holding single large cap, small cap, bond, and international funds makes more sense.

Question 176: **Which is better—load or no-load funds?**

Load funds charge commissions of up to 8 percent (usually less) to purchase the fund. The load can be charged either up-front, upon sale, or sometime during ownership, and it is mainly paid as commission to the financial professional selling the fund with a portion left for administration. Four or five percent taken out of your investment up-front is a hefty blow, taking a while to recover through compounding. Many funds today prefer the no-load approach, where commissions are essentially pulled out of investment value. No-load funds do spread the impact across time and across more investors, but they are far from transparent. It is more difficult to know exactly what the fund is charging its investors. Generally, most investors are better off with no-load funds, but a good load fund is better than a bad no-load fund.

Question 177: **Fund listings in the newspaper show Class A, B, and C shares for many mutual fund groups. Are these grades, or what?**

These letters do not represent grades, but rather load structure for load funds. "A" shares charge the load up-front with a smaller 12-b-1 marketing and distribution fee and are the most common type. "B" shares charge a back-end redemption fee and a higher 12-b-1 fee, and "C" shares typically spread the load over the first few years with a 12-b-1 and other management fees. Which is best? The "A" approach takes a big cut up-front, taking money that could otherwise grow and compound off the table. The "B" approach is attractive because it defers this expense, but since the redemption fee is a percentage, you may pay more later if the investment grows. The "C" approach is attractive because it spreads the cost, but the costs are often higher. It's sort of a "pick your poison" debate, and many investors choose to avoid the tough choice altogether by buying no-load funds, which effectively spread costs over the course of ownership—though again these costs might be higher and might interfere with the power of compounding.

Question 178: **What are the major tax implications of mutual fund investing? How can I avoid tax surprises?**

Mutual funds are *pass-through entities,* that is, realized earnings and losses are passed through to be accounted for on your own income taxes. Income received in the form of dividends and interest on fund holdings are passed through as ordinary dividend income to you, as are capital gains realized during the year. Unfortunately, most funds pass through their gains at the end of the year. Suppose you buy a fund in November that has realized a lot of gains in its portfolio during the year. You will pay a higher price, or *net asset value,* for the shares, and you'll also be accountable for the capital gains realized through the year paid out at year end. Frequent buying and selling, or *portfolio turnover,* produces realized gains, and investors seeking to avoid capital gains taxes seek funds with low turnover. The good news: recent capital gains rate reductions have reduced the tax bite, and it's a nonissue for funds used in retirement or tax-deferred college savings accounts.

Question 179: **How should I select a fund?**

Obviously, the answer is complex. The short answer: investors should look at fund objectives, track record, and expenses.

The first step: do a fund's objectives and style match your goals? Growth, aggressive growth, value, income, "contrarian" performance opposite to the market, or international exposure? There is no sure measure, but stated fund objectives and core fund holdings help. Look at the fund company Web site or use the Yahoo!Finance or Morningstar portals (*finance.yahoo.com* and *www.morningstar.com*).

Performance assessment runs two ways. The first compares to overall market and sector performance; the second compares to risk. Check how the fund has performed against the major market indices and, in particular, against a similar basket of stocks (large cap fund vs. all large cap stocks). Morningstar compares performance to peer group stocks; these ratings appear in some newspaper tables (the *New York Times,* for example).

The *Sharpe's Ratio* compares performance to fund volatility, a risk measure, and can be found in financial portals mentioned previously. The lower the ratio, the better.

Finally, you should review costs—all costs—including management, 12-b-1, operating, loads, and other. Most information sources gather these into an *expense ratio.* Today's investing climate makes it imperative to get value for your investing dollar.

Question 180: **My fund company has received bad press lately. How do I decide if it's time to pull out?**

Recently uncovered mutual fund scandals have hurt trust in what was once a staid, solid way for Americans to invest. Put simply, some mutual fund managers started to act for their own interest—and that of certain clients—in letting some trade the funds after hours and in other ways contrary to holder interest. While harming trust, the effects aren't extensive and don't suggest an immediate exit from the fund or fund company. The real decision is whether the fund management is working for you and in your best interests. Good performance, open and honest management communications, and contrition from involved managers are all good signs. Still, if a fund or fund company makes you nervous and you can change without substantial financial penalty, there are lots of choices. Simply put, why should you lose sleep at night?

Question 181: **What is an exchange traded fund? What are the pros and cons?**

Exchange Traded Funds (ETFs) are a rapidly emerging alternative to traditional mutual funds. Like mutual funds, they are investment pools set up to buy and sell securities. But unlike mutual funds, shares are traded on regular stock exchanges, mostly the American Stock Exchange (NASDAQ/AMEX). There are about 140 actively traded ETFs today, and the number is growing rapidly. Some are set up to track U.S. and international stock indexes; some track specific business sectors (see Question 182).

ETFs offer a convenient, inexpensive, and nimble way to diversify an investment portfolio. They offer visibility. It is easy to view ETF holdings; one way is through the ETF portal at Yahoo!Finance *(finance.yahoo.com)*.

Most ETFs aren't actively managed, and so you are more exposed to the movements of the market. They don't offer the customer service features of many mutual funds. However, some of the newer fund offerings are actively managed.

Question 182: **What kinds of ETFs are available?**

ETFs are set up to track various stock indices or sectors of the market, including international markets. *Index ETFs* are inactively managed and set up to track a major index. The ever-more-popular Standard & Poor's 500 Depository Receipts (SPDR) and the NASDAQ 100 Index (QQQ) ETFs are examples. They offer a way to participate at minimal cost—a brokerage commission and expenses running less than 0.20 percent per year.

Sector ETFs track business sectors like energy, health care, or financial services. These funds have limited management in selecting the twenty or thirty largest or most important stocks in the sector. Expenses are low, and these vehicles allow the small investor to play in specific sectors of their choice and to rotate investments. It is likely that ETF choices will grow rapidly as the simplicity and popularity of these investments expands.

Question 183: **How should I use ETFs in my portfolio?**

ETFs are a handy alternative to mutual funds. They allow large and small investors to set up all or part of their portfolio to track a market or market sector. With their low costs and visibility, ETFs make sense as a low-risk "buy and hold" investment for small investors with limited funds to invest. For larger investors, ETFs are a way to tie part of a portfolio to market performance, allowing more active management of the rest of the portfolio. They are also a handy way to gain international exposure or rotate investments between market sectors falling in and out of favor. Since they are funds containing many stocks, investors are cautioned to be patient for results.

Question 184: **Describe the different ways to invest in real estate and their pros and cons.**

The major ways to invest in real estate are direct investments, real estate investment trusts (REITs), and limited partnerships.

Direct investments include buying your own residence or rental property. Such investments have a good track record for appreciation and give an opportunity to add sweat equity value but also can bring costs, time commitments, and headaches that some fail to anticipate. They are tied to specific locations and are far from diversified.

REITs are like mutual funds specializing in real estate, usually a sector of the real estate market like commercial, residential, rental property, or shopping centers. Some specialize in geographic regions. Like a mutual fund, you buy shares and capture returns as dividends or capital gains. While these vehicles offer an easy and more diversified way to invest, you may not know exactly what they own or how your money is being managed.

Limited partnerships are equity ownerships in a specific portfolio of real estate, mainly tailored to larger investors looking for tax advantages in addition to investment performance. They are beyond the scope of most average investors.

Question 185: All my friends seem to be making money with their real estate investments. They brag about easy gains. Am I missing something or are they?

Driven by low interest rates, strong demand, low supply in key markets, and gains in household formation, real estate indeed has been a good investment in the past five to ten years. So your friends probably have made money.

Since they can borrow 80 percent of the value and sometimes more, the rate of return on their invested capital may be especially high. A $200,000 house bought with $40,000 down, appreciating to $300,000, suggests a $100,000 profit on $40,000, or a 250 percent return. This is worth bragging about, but it still must be looked at in full. How much expense did they incur maintaining the property, paying mortgage interest and taxes, finding tenants (for rental property), and so forth? How much risk did they take? How long did it take? How much capital gains tax will they pay, if it's a rental property?

The sober analysis: if they made $100,000 "face value" on the property in eight years, with $20,000 in expenses and $12,000 in capital gains taxes, they really made $68,000, or 170 percent. On a compounded growth basis, that works out to 13 percent per year—not bad at all, but perhaps not enough to be the life of the cocktail party.

Question 186: **What are equity options, and what should I know about them?**

Equity options are risk transfer mechanisms where owners of stock can sell or buy the right to acquire a stock by a fixed date at a fixed price. *Call options* allow another investor to *buy* that stock from them at a fixed price by a fixed date; *put options* allow the investor to *sell* their stock to another investor at a fixed price by a fixed date. For that right, the selling investor collects a *premium*—the price of the option.

If an investor holds 100 shares of XYZ Inc., they can sell you the right to buy those shares from them (a call), perhaps at $20 by the third Friday (the usual settlement date) of April. If the stock currently is at $19.25 ("out of the money"), the premium might be $1.00, meaning that each *contract*, which is to transfer 100 shares, brings the investor (and costs you) $100. The premium will be more or less depending on the *time to expiration*, the current price of the stock compared to the *strike price* of $20, and *share price volatility*.

Call option sellers are generating short-term income from their holdings at the expense of potential future gains; call buyers are trying to achieve big gains for relatively small investments. Call sellers reduce risk by turning uncertain potential to cash; call buyers risk losing their premium, but that amount only. Put buyers insulate their portfolios against major downturns; put sellers are using cash on the sidelines to generate more cash and capitalize on overly negative feelings about a stock.

Question 187: **I thought all option plays were risky. Right or wrong?**

Many people immediately think "risk" when they hear the word "option." But in fact, options can be used to reduce portfolio risk and generate certain cash against uncertain market performance. Selling *covered call options* at a higher strike price—that is, collecting a premium for letting someone buy your stock at a price higher than today's—is a good way to collect cash. You get the premium, plus the advance to the strike price, at the expense of losing potential for a larger but still more uncertain gain. Buying puts on portfolio holdings reduces risk of a major market downturn or company "blowup," but this time you are paying out the cash—analogous to buying insurance on your stock portfolio. Both of these transactions reduce risk; selling covered calls has the additional advantage of generating cash, although the downside risk is still there. The mechanics are a bit complex and should be studied by ordinary investors before jumping in. These tools are available and used by "main street" investors.

Question 188: **Scenario: I have $4,500 to invest. What should I do?**

First, we must assume these savings are "free" to invest—that is, they aren't required as part of your day-to-day finances or emergency fund. Further, let's assume these assets are outside your retirement plan, which, if a 401(k)-style plan, has its own set of specific investment choices.

The amount involved may be enough to justify setting up a brokerage account but be careful about fees and minimum balances. Through a discount brokerage account (you don't have enough to interest a full-service broker), you can buy individual stocks, mutual funds, or exchange traded funds. ETFs are probably the best choice in this scenario, for they offer market performance with relatively low costs and allow some foray into specific business sectors, such as health care, technology, or even more aggressive biotech investments. With this amount, it may make sense to stick with a broader market ETF, such as the SPDR (S&P 500) fund. If you are young and looking for more aggressive growth with the risk that entails, one of the more "sexy," or dynamic, sectors makes sense, and you may have enough for two separate funds, probably not more. Individual stocks probably don't make sense at this point.

The other alternative is to invest directly with a mutual fund family, eliminating brokerage costs and providing the fund switching and customer service you might need. Mutual funds offer monthly payment plans, helping you save and grow your asset.

Question 189: **Scenario: I am a thirty-year-old novice investor with $50,000 to invest, mostly from personal savings and a small inheritance. Where should I invest, and what should I avoid?**

You're in good position to start building an investment base, if you haven't already. At this point in life, some liquidity is important—three to six months' salary or so, but you can afford to invest the majority for the long term. Being young, you can afford to take some risk.

You should think in terms of a portfolio with some "base" market-tracking investments like ETFs, mutual funds, or "blue chip" dividend-paying stocks. To that, you might add some individual stocks chosen to capitalize on growth-for-value opportunities. The mix of these investments depends in part on how actively you wish to manage your portfolio.

There are at least two things to avoid. One is overconcentration in your employer's own shares or even in the same industry, a common mistake in 401(k) plans. A downturn can hit you twice. Also, at this stage, most bond investments don't make sense, as inflation tempers returns. If you're not yet comfortable as an investor, it's a good time to learn, and you might want to use an advisor or find a discount broker offering some advice, at least for the short term.

Question 190: **Scenario: I have $100,000 invested, mainly in long-term growth stocks and index funds. I may be headed for a period of income instability. How do I rebalance my portfolio to generate more income?**

This is the sort of switch many investors need to make during different life stages—either to protect income or provide for college education and the like. The first step is to reframe investing objectives. Most investors in this class want 8 to 10 percent returns for the long term and even more and are willing to forego current returns and take more risk to get there. The new objective requires downsized expectations—for instance, to 5 to 7 percent per year—and playing the game to meet or slightly exceed market performance. There are many ways to do this; here are a few:

- Keep a "core" portfolio to track major market indexes—in that way, you maintain at least some market participation.
- Look for a few dividend-paying, value-oriented stocks still preserving some growth potential. Bank stocks might be a good example.
- Learn to sell covered call options on some of your individual stock investments to generate short-term cash. You can also sell S&P 500 and other index calls to generate cash. Read up on and practice this before venturing too deep, and a broker or advisor familiar with these tools can help.

PART III

Keeping the Ship on Course: Avoiding Financial Surprises

Chapter **11**

PROTECTING LIFE AND HEALTH

Now we switch gears from creating and growing wealth to *protecting* it. Nothing can derail the wealth train faster than unexpected, catastrophic events that wipe out the assets or income supporting you and your future. The possibility of adverse events is *risk,* and the practice of guarding against risk is *risk management.*

Risk management implies planning for all types of risk. Yes, there's a risk that your bagel toaster might break—what do you do? You may decide to buy an extended warranty—insurance—but why? You can simply replace it or *absorb the risk.* You may *reduce risk* by using it less often or *avoid risk* by not having it at all. Similarly, in life, you may *reduce risk* by wearing seat belts and *avoid risk* by not going skydiving. Although reducing and avoiding risks might prolong your life, there is no guarantee that something won't happen. If it does, it is indeed a catastrophe—financially and otherwise. For such big risks that you can't eliminate, you *transfer the risk*—that is, buy insurance. This chapter covers risk-transferring insurance for life, health, and ability to produce income, while Chapter 12 covers insurance for the major assets in your life—your property.

Question 191: **Why should I buy life insurance?**

The most obvious reason is to protect the finances of your family or household in case of your untimely demise. If you die early, expenses will continue, and large obligations such as mortgages still need to be met. Obligations may even increase. What if you were the only earner receiving family health insurance coverage through your employer? That will need to be replaced, too.

Another reason to buy insurance today, even if you don't have a family to protect, is to insure future insurance availability if your health declines. You must be in good health to qualify for some policies or to get preferred rates. Buying a permanent policy today guarantees having insurance tomorrow. Taking advantage of employer group plans requires no physical examination now or later—even to increase the insured amount. Term policies can be bought for long coverage periods; it is easier to renew policies than to start from scratch. In general, it's good to "get under the umbrella," buying insurance you might not need this minute.

Question 192: **How much life insurance do I need?**

Most financial advisors use two approaches to determine insurance needs. The *obligations* approach measures how much your household will need to carry on—housing, expenses, big-ticket items, college expenses, and other special needs. Future income potential from remaining family members is subtracted to arrive at an insured amount. The *income replacement* approach estimates how much income you would have produced if still alive adjusted for time value of money. Both approaches are complicated but valid.

As a simple rule of thumb, most advisors recommend insuring income-producing family members for about ten times their annual income as a starting point. Other factors may suggest greater or lesser need, for instance, assets owned or special expenses.

Question 193: **What are the advantages of group life insurance?**

Group life insurance is typically offered through employers or professional organizations. As the name implies, the insurance company looks at the insured as a pool, not individuals, and rates the policy accordingly. This means lower rates since administrative costs are less. Moreover, you don't have to qualify individually for the insurance. The group rate already assumes some high-risk individuals are in the group so that the insurance company doesn't spend extra money to check everyone out. This means that you do far less to qualify for the insurance; there is no physical exam, for instance. Most groups allow adding coverage whenever you want, still with specific qualification waived. So group policies have advantages, especially for high-risk individuals.

Question 194: **What different types of life insurance can I buy?**

The two main types of life insurance are *term* and *permanent*. *Term* insurance lasts for a defined period of time; you pay premiums over this time and receive a defined benefit upon death. If you don't die during the term period, the policy simply goes away. Term insurance is typically available for one-, five-, ten-, fifteen-, and twenty-year periods. Level term policies spread premiums evenly through the term instead of raising premiums each year according to mortality risk.

    Permanent insurance, once bought, lasts until you die, whenever that might be. Permanent insurance pays a defined amount upon death but also accumulates *cash value* for each year you don't die; it is actually an asset in addition to coverage. Permanent insurance comes in whole life, universal life, and variable universal life forms. *Whole life,* the most basic form, requires a fixed premium payment for a defined number of years with a predefined cash value accumulation. *Universal life* is a form of whole life allowing flexible premium payments; your cash value and death benefit vary according to how much is paid in. *Variable universal life* incorporates an investment component: cash value and death benefits vary according to your payments and investment performance.

Question 195: **Do I buy term or permanent insurance?**

This is a common debate in personal finance. Do you buy term insurance, simply providing coverage, or go for the more expensive permanent insurance? Term insurance provides coverage only for the defined period and is protection in its most pure form. It requires significantly lower cash outlays. For those who need coverage and coverage only, term insurance is usually enough.

But what happens when the term is over? If you buy a twenty-year level term policy at age thirty-five, you'll get good coverage until age fifty-five. Then you're back into the insurance market again, facing several times as much in premiums. Worse yet, your health may have deteriorated so that you may not be insurable at all. You have accumulated no cash value; those premiums you paid are gone.

These are the typical arguments offered by insurance agents and permanent insurance proponents. Permanent insurance is just that—it is permanent. You never have to qualify again for insurance, and premiums don't rise. Further, you accumulate cash value, a handy forced savings tool for many people. But careful analysis usually reveals that the asset accumulation part of permanent insurance doesn't accumulate assets as fast as you can through normal investing. Why? Because something must be set aside to cover death benefits, not to mention agent commissions and other expenses. Term proponents recommend buying term insurance and investing the premium difference separately.

Who's right? It really depends on your situation. If you're healthy and have insurance needs that really last only a defined amount of time, the *"term + investing" approach* is probably better. You simply may not need so much insurance coverage once your children are grown, other assets are accumulated, and your home is paid off.

The bottom line: insure the need and don't get caught by tempting sales pitches.

Question 196: **What is the best way to buy life insurance?**

The best way to buy life insurance is usually through your employer, if there is a group plan available. If no insurance benefit is available or if you want more insurance, there are two choices: buy from an insurance agent or buy online.

Because of its investment features, permanent insurance forms (whole life, universal, or variable universal life) are only offered through licensed insurance professionals; these products aren't available online. Choosing an agent can be tricky. There are a lot of "sharks" out there attracted by the lure of high commissions, and it is usually a very "salesy" experience. Find an agent you can trust through a personal referral or financial advisor and make sure they take the time to explain the features and benefits of each policy clearly and in understandable terms.

Term insurance buyers find the Internet attractive if armed with a little knowledge (if not, most insurer Web sites offer good educational materials). Web insurance portals like SelectQuote *(www.selectquote.com)* and Insweb *(www.insweb.com)* give handy, easy-to-navigate comparative quotes from high-grade companies and offer modest premium savings. Of course, term insurance is also available through your insurance agent.

Question 197: **My insurance agent talks about add-on "riders" to life policies. I get easily confused by the jargon and buzzwords. What do I really need to know?**

Most likely you've heard about some or all of the following.

- *Renewability.* Some term life policies—and importantly, health and disability policies—offer guaranteed renewability. That is, you can renew regardless of changes in your health— valuable if concerned about your long-term health.
- *Premium waiver.* If you become incapacitated or chronically ill, the last thing you want is unpaid insurance bills hanging over your head. Premium waivers stop premiums under certain conditions, though may add more than you'd like to your bill.
- *Convertibility.* Some term policies can be changed to permanent forms, a way of guaranteeing renewability and

useful if your financial situation or needs change. Typically, it can only be done during the first few years of a term.

- *Accidental death coverage* adds additional benefits if your death is an accident. There may also be benefits for partial disability or dismemberment.

Although these features sound nice, their cost must be evaluated rationally against the base premium cost and against other ways to protect against the risk. As with cars, such options are often more profitable for the insurance company and lucrative for agents.

Question 198: **Should I consider buying life insurance for my children?**

Many insurance agents suggest policies for children, and indeed the low premiums driven by low mortality risk are compelling. For permanent insurance buyers, it's a way to get started early.

Some may feel the loss of a child can be made a tiny bit less painful by a substantial insurance payment. But really, there is no financial need; in fact, the loss of a child reduces financial requirements. There is simply no financial justification to buy term insurance for a child. As for permanent insurance, it's probably better to invest separately to take advantage of the long compounding period.

Question 199: **In general, what are the tax implications of life insurance?**

When disaster strikes, it provides at least a degree of comfort to know that the benefit check arrives quickly and is completely income-tax free. Why? Because premiums were paid with after-tax dollars; so taxes have essentially already been paid. However, insurance proceeds are taxable for *estate tax* purposes unless the insurance policy has been transferred into a special insurance trust (the details are beyond our scope here—ask your advisor). As estate tax exemptions are growing, such tax doesn't affect many.

Earnings on permanent insurance forms are taxable only on a deferred basis. Earnings compound favorably without taxation. This makes such policies, particularly stock-market-driven variable universal life policies, attractive for some investors. Those who have sufficient income and have maximized other retirement-plan contributions might consider variable universal life as a way to add to tax-deferred retirement savings.

Question 200: **What factors drive life insurance cost? If I have high risk factors, what should I do?**

Life insurance premiums are driven by age, health, habits, and family history. The impact of age is obvious. According to mortality tables used in the insurance industry, at age twenty-five approximately two males (one female) per 1,000 die, rising to four (four also for females) at age forty-five; twenty-five (fifteen females) at age sixty-five; 152 (116 females) at age eighty-five. So, pure coverage term premiums expand dramatically as you get older.

Insurance companies usually offer *preferred, standard,* and *high-risk rates.* Health, habits, and family history become important in classifying individual policies. Smokers will pay more, and physical examination results play a key role. Family history—both parents dying before sixty of natural causes, for example—can cause loss of preferred status. The difference between preferred, standard, and high-risk rates is large; a fall from preferred to standard can double term life insurance rates. People with high risk factors should look for companies more tolerant of those risk factors. Insurers view different health risks and especially more nebulous factors like family history differently.

Question 201: **Is the choice of life insurance companies important?**

The TV ads are all compelling—own a piece of the rock, etc. Most companies offer largely the same assortment of term and permanent insurance products. Some may offer slightly different features, and it is worthwhile to shop for premiums. Many now offer other investment products and advice. But the core question is: will they be around fifty years from now when you want to cash out your permanent insurance policy? Will they be able to pay a claim easily and quickly ten years from now when your family so badly needs it?

Insurance companies should be judged by their permanence, which translates to financial stability, and to an extent, for their customer service. Fortunately, it is relatively easy to assess stability; a rating service known as A.M. Best rates companies on an A/B/C/D scale. These ratings are relatively easy to find, and you should look for "A" and better companies. Customer service is more nebulous but starts with your agent. Is your agent helpful and cooperative? Are explanations easy to get and understandable? Are you comfortable? This part is a judgment call.

Question 202: What are some of the disadvantages in buying whole or universal life?

The decision to buy any type of permanent insurance should be approached carefully, for it is, well, permanent. Perhaps not completely, for you can cash out of a policy and stop paying premiums, thus effectively ending the policy. But early termination fees can make that costly.

Examine the agent's sales presentation very carefully. The product is complex, the terminology is daunting, and agents stand to make high commissions on permanent policies. Long-term performance, particularly for variable universal life products, can be adjusted to look very attractive by choosing high and unrealistic return rates. Sure, you can end up with a couple of million dollars with a 10 percent effective annual return—but how likely is that, especially when the insurance company is taking some for expenses and payouts? Make sure to see the numbers with realistic and worst-case scenarios. Be sure you understand everything (and read and ask questions until you do) before making an informed decision.

Question 203: **Scenario: I am thirty-eight, married with no children, and have $50,000 annual income as an employee. How much, and what kind of insurance should I get?**

At this stage of life, your insurance needs are fairly basic. The first question: can your spouse replace your income? Then, what expenses would you expect to have? Normal expenses? Mortgage? At this point, it's a pencil-and-paper exercise, and the rule of thumb of replacing ten years worth of income is a good place to start, though you might need less if your spouse has earning potential.

The next question concerns the future. Do you expect to have children? If so, that expands the required amount and also makes it more important that you stay insurable while they are still dependent. Buy insurance—even if you don't think you need it now. Your employer's group life plan is the best place to start shopping. You may get some coverage for free, but additional amounts are cheap and can be had without questions. You may choose not to insure your entire need this way. What happens if you lose your job? A supplemental term life policy with a long level term of twenty years makes sense.

Permanent insurance may be a good idea if you've maxed out other retirement savings vehicles (unlikely at this income level) or if you are trying to build wealth and have trouble saving otherwise. But for most people, a long level term insurance policy probably is cheapest and makes the most sense. Buy the most you can reasonably afford, especially if your survivors will have a difficult time replacing your income.

Question 204: **Disability insurance—do I need it?**

Disability insurance replaces a portion of your income should you remain living but become unable to earn income. Do you need it? Statistics show disability is much more likely than death; the average worker is two to three times as likely to have a disability claim than a life insurance claim during their working life. Like life insurance, disability produces income for your household when you can't.

Question 205: **My employer offers me "any occupation" disability coverage. Is this good, or is there something better?**

There are two kinds of disability coverage. *Own occupation* coverage pays if you become unable to perform in your own profession. *Any occupation* coverage pays only if you are unable to perform work for income at all. While any occupation insurance sounds better, on further examination you must demonstrate complete disability, that is, you cannot work in any capacity before collecting. This is a stringent test. These policies only pay with severe disabilities and so are less attractive than own occupation alternatives. Doctors, airline pilots, and other highly skilled professionals tend to buy own occupation coverage since they want coverage if they become unable to perform in their own specialized profession.

Question 206: **How much disability coverage do I need?**

Most disability policies promise to pay some portion of your income in the event of disability—50, 60, or 75 percent. Full income replacement policies are expensive and are usually not offered through employers. There is some coverage through the Social Security system. But the coverage is limited, and the disability must be severe. Many states offer limited disability coverage as well, but again disabilities must pass stringent criteria for one to collect. Most disability coverage also comes with a waiting period; that is, you can only collect after a defined period of time elapses.

Disability needs depend on your income needs, current assets, and alternatives for producing household income if you become disabled. Can your spouse replace your income? Can you do something else if you become injured in an auto accident? Remember, income needs often rise during periods of disability. What about uncovered medical expenses and insurance deductibles? Who is going to mow your lawn, and how much will it cost? You may need more than you think.

Question 207: **What are the main types of health coverage available today? What is "managed care"?**

Health coverage comes in two major types, each of which may be covered by some form of health insurance. *Managed care* consists of a set of services managed by a health care providing corporation. *Private care* has no intermediary; you simply choose your doctor directly.

Managed care organizations hire or contract with medical professionals to provide certain services at a certain price. Health insurers finance health care through a variety of insurance products but do not deliver the care. *Health Maintenance Organizations* (HMOs) provide both; they offer medical care services and an insurance package to pay for them. Since costs are controlled directly, especially with in-house HMOs like Kaiser Permanente, HMOs usually provide the lowest cost but offer the least flexibility to choose among doctors and service alternatives.

Preferred Provider Organizations (PPOs) are a looser confederation of contracted care providers. Patients can choose among a network of care providers and can use out-of-network providers with this coverage, if they are willing to pay a higher deductible. Typically, the care provider is separate from the insurer. PPOs are somewhat more expensive but offer the patient greater choice.

Question 208: **What is the difference between "deductibles," "co-insurance," and "copays"?**

A copay, or *copayment,* is a charge paid by the insured with each incident of medical coverage. If you have a $20 doctor copay, you pay $20 for each visit to a doctor. Copayment for hospital and emergency room services may differ, and some plans may offer a different copayment for preventative services like a routine physical. Generally, the higher the copay, the lower the cost of insurance.

Coinsurance represents the amount you pay as a percentage of the costs of each event above and beyond the copayment. Typical policies require you to pay for 20 percent of any service, while the insurer pays the other 80 percent. The higher the coinsurance, the lower the insurance premium.

Finally, the *deductible* represents a minimum floor below which the insured pays 100 percent of costs. Deductibles may be set for individuals or combined for a family. If you have a policy with a $500 individual deductible, a $20 copay, and 20 percent coinsurance, you would pay all costs up to $500/year. Beyond $500, you would pay 20 percent of each medical bill plus a $20 copay for each visit. Copayments typically do apply toward deductible amounts.

Question 209: **Every time I'm confronted with health decisions, like during open enrollment, I am bewildered by the technology. What features should I look for in my health plan?**

Each choice has important cost factors and features. Major cost factors include deductibles, copayments, and coinsurance (see Question 208) and the portion of the premium you'll have to pay if it is an employer-sponsored plan. Typically, you'll have choices among these cost factors; higher premiums will buy you lower copays, deductibles, and coinsurance amounts.

Key plan features include prescription drug coverage (is there any, and what are deductibles, coinsurance, and copays?), maternity coverage, and preventative care provisions. If you choose a high-deductible plan, do you still get coverage for physical examinations? Does prescription drug coverage limit the coverage for new or proprietary medications? If you're in an individual plan (not employer provided), what are the renewability provisions? You need to shop carefully through the matrix of benefits and costs and make a careful decision about what's right for you. Most employers have advisors to help navigate the maze.

Question 210: **Why has health insurance become such a hot issue recently?**

Health care costs and health insurance premiums have risen at a staggering rate, almost 49 percent in the 2000–2004 period; yet family incomes have risen only 8 percent during that period. The gap is being made up in part by employers passing large chunks of the cost of health insurance premiums to employees. The only good news is that these increased premiums are generally paid with before-tax dollars, and most self-employed can deduct 100 percent of health insurance premiums. With that said, there are almost 50 million uninsured people in the United States. People are living longer and coming down with more complex, longer-lasting diseases. Further, with the demise of traditional retirement pensions, people must protect their assets from the financial catastrophe of a major illness. For most of these issues there is no improvement in sight.

Question 211: **How can I keep health insurance costs down?**

Whether an individual policy or an employer plan, health insurance costs can be kept down by choosing higher deductibles, copayments, and coinsurance amounts (see Question 208). This applies both to care services and prescription drugs. All options should be examined. Some families, particularly those with individual insurance coverage, choose less expensive HMO coverage for children and PPO coverage for themselves, as children typically need more frequent but less serious care. Putting an individual policy in the youngest adult's name is another way to save a few dollars. The advent of *health savings accounts* (HSAs), an expansion of *medical savings accounts* (MSAs) already available to self-employed individuals, will help. These plans, currently being implemented in the tax code, allow individuals to reduce health insurance costs by increasing deductibles and covering them through a personally owned pretax savings account. They are particularly attractive to healthier individuals and families.

HSAs are currently being promoted by the federal government and many financial and health insurance advisors as a way for *all* workers—not just self-employed workers—to make health-care costs more affordable. This becomes especially true as employers pay less and less of the tab. HSAs are attractive for funding increased subscriber health costs across a wide range of health issues, including eye and dental care. But they have the added attraction of being a supplemental retirement plan, as funds not used for health care can be invested and used for retirement, much like a deductible IRA. Finally, as MSAs were limited to self-employed individuals, plan choices were limited and administrative costs were high. But as HSAs become mainstream, we're likely to see more and better choices for managed individual health-care accounts. In sum, HSAs are probably the biggest—perhaps only—good news on the health-care cost front in a long time.

Question 212: **I am self-employed. What are my options?**

Self-employed individuals face unique health care challenges. Typical health plans, can cost more than $1,000/month for a family. Premiums are now 100 percent deductible, but it is still a substantial expense.

There are two paths to lowering these costs. First, if you can get into a group-based coverage somehow, that helps. Group plans are priced considering lower administrative costs and do not require individual underwriting—that is, qualification—of plan participants. Some insurance companies are writing group coverage for firms with as few as four or five employees, and some self-employed individuals may find group coverage through a professional or trade organization. Group plans are essential if you have some preexisting health situation that may hinder qualification.

The other path is to get a special *major medical policy* coupled to a *medical savings account*, or MSA. The major medical coverage may have very high deductibles, up to $5,000 per family, but the MSA allows you to save up to $3,000 before taxes to pay this amount and cover other health-related expenses (even things like eyeglasses). If you don't use the MSA savings, it can be withdrawn without a penalty after age fifty-nine-and-a-half; so it acts as a supplemental retirement plan.

Question 213: **What is COBRA, and how does it work?**

COBRA stands for Consolidated Omnibus Budget Reconciliation Act of 1986, a piece of umbrella legislation allowing employees to continue group health coverage for a period of time after termination. The act was designed to allow employees to change jobs or try different forms of employment without having to qualify for and pay for individual coverage immediately. Companies with twenty or more employees must offer COBRA coverage, which allows the insured to pay for insurance at the previous group rate usually for eighteen months after termination. COBRA coverage is not free but makes coverage available at reduced rates. COBRA saves money and maintains insurability. Most individual health insurance providers will accept a COBRA transferee without a physical exam or qualification if they had previous coverage for long enough.

Question 214: **Does it make sense to get dental insurance?**

Dental insurance typically has high deductibles and is relatively expensive. Moreover, even the most expensive dental procedures cost just a few hundred dollars. There is no catastrophic event to insure against as there is with health, life, or disability. If an employer offers dental insurance, that's good. But most families are better served to put the premiums into savings (especially pretax medical savings plans through work or medical savings accounts if self employed).

Question 215: **What is long-term-care insurance? Do I need it?**

Long-term-care insurance is designed to insure against the risk of frailty in old age. You might need extended care for so-called activities of daily living—eating, dressing, cleaning—over a long period of time. Nursing homes and other forms of extended care are very expensive, running $25,000 to $100,000/year depending on the type of care and location. Average long-term care periods run one and a half to two years. But people are living longer, and the chance of needing such care at some point has grown.

Most financial advisors recommend long-term-care insurance if you have a mid-range asset base at retirement—between $100,000 and $1 million. Why? People with less are poor enough (or will be soon) to qualify for state aid programs such as Medicaid. People with sufficient assets can self-insure, that is, pay most costs and have enough left over for other retirement needs.

Chapter **12**

PROTECTING PROPERTY

While life and disability insurance primarily protect income, property/casualty insurance protects from financial loss suffered through adverse events involving property and from loss of the property itself. For example, auto insurance covers damage you might inflict on someone else with your car. Depending on coverage, it also protects you from the loss of the car itself. Homeowner's insurance protects in the same way, although the loss protection component is more important because of high asset value. Property/casualty insurance should be purchased for auto, home, and other major assets.

Question 216: How does property/casualty insurance fit into my overall financial plan?

Property/casualty insurance—mainly auto and homeowners' policies—protect against financial catastrophe caused by loss of the property or by damage caused to others with or on the property. These policies cover home and car contents, too; so they end up covering most of a household's assets. Like health insurance, there are choices ranging from full coverage to high-deductible policies designed to cover only catastrophic events with large premium savings. For most people, higher-deductible forms make sense since it is the catastrophe you're guarding against, not every $100 bit of damage that might occur. A special form known as *umbrella* coverage goes beyond standard policies to cover very large liability exposure—$1 million and upward—combined for all owned property. With today's litigation, umbrella coverage is relatively inexpensive protection, especially if you have something to protect or unusual risk factors like teenage drivers.

Question 217: **How much auto insurance do I/we need?**

It's important to understand the different parts of an auto policy. Most auto insurance policies have liability, collision, and comprehensive components with an assortment of "extras" added on.

The liability component covers harm or damage you might inflict on someone else in an accident. Most liability coverage is divided into three components: a per-individual, a per-accident, and a property damage dollar amount. Thus, a "100–300–50" policy covers up to $100,000 in damages inflicted upon another person, $300,000 in damages for all persons involved, and $50,000 covering the value of someone else's car or other property involved. Most advisors recommend buying as much liability coverage as possible. Liability coverage is expensive, but increased amounts of coverage are relatively cheap. It may cost only 10 percent more to go from $300,000 per accident to $500,000 per accident in coverage. With the increased value of today's cars, property damage coverage should be $100,000 or more if possible. Even if you have little wealth to protect, some courts "garnish" or attach wages to settle damages, particularly if negligence was involved in the accident.

While liability covers the interests of others involved in the accident, collision and comprehensive coverages protect your own vehicle. Collision insurance protects against loss or damage of your vehicle in an accident. Comprehensive insurance covers loss to your vehicle in nonaccident events—storm damage, theft, fire, and so forth. Deductibles usually apply to these coverages. You can choose deductibles, and depending on the value of the vehicle, may choose to go without these coverages altogether.

Aside from liability, collision, and comprehensive coverages, most auto policies carry mandatory coverage against damage inflicted upon you by uninsured motorists, and they may have other add-on coverages for medical payments for you and vehicle passengers, vehicle towing, and car rental in the event of damage to your vehicle. Some of these extras may be quite expensive when considering value of coverage actually received.

Question 218: I drive a 1994 Ford Explorer. Should I buy collision and comprehensive insurance?

Collision and comprehensive insurance protect the value of your vehicle and provide *secondary* protection when you drive someone else's vehicle with permission (their insurance comes first). Your vehicle has probably depreciated so that even a total loss would bring a settlement of $3,000 or less; so you may decide these coverages aren't necessary. Premiums may run 10 to 20 percent of that amount—a large cash outlay for modest protection. Check with your agent to get premium costs and estimated settlement value.

You may choose these coverages if you rent vehicles frequently. Typically your coverages apply to rented vehicles, so without collision coverage on your own car, you probably don't have it when you rent. Supplemental coverage available from car rental companies is expensive; it may be cheaper to carry collision and comprehensive insurance yourself. Notably, you're protected for the full value of the rental car less your deductible—even if your car is worth only $3,000.

Question 219: How can I lower my auto insurance costs?

A common question asked each time the renewal notice arrives. You consider yourself a safe driver with a good record—and yet that bill keeps going up and up. Insurance companies remind us that liability exposure and the cost to repair or replace cars continue to rise steadily. Today's cars have expensive gadgets and are set up for manufacturing—not repair—efficiency. So what can you do?

Most advisors recommend against taking short cuts on liability coverage. The places to look are collision, comprehensive, and so-called extra coverages, like medical, towing, and rental car coverage if your car is wrecked. By raising collision deductibles, you can save without adding much risk to your overall finances. Ask yourself how much you're willing to pay for that first $500 of insurance. It probably isn't worth $100/year, is it? The extra coverages can also be quite expensive; towing insurance that might pay $300 at most may cost $20 to $30/year.

Also, you may be eligible for discounts not even considered—for a good driving record, carrying homeowner's insurance through the same company, and even membership in a professional organization. The bottom line: check with your agent, review each line item, and don't forget to ask how driving a less expensive vehicle might help. Make sure that you don't cause an accident or get traffic citations; cost will increase with little to be done about it.

Question 220: **Every time I rent a car, the agency pitches hard to sell Collision Damage Waivers, Loss Damage Waivers, and so forth. Are these necessary?**

Typically, the coverages you buy for your own vehicle apply when you rent a car. So you are covered for liability, collision damage, and the nonaccident events covered by comprehensive insurance. Although most auto policies are standardized, it is worth checking with your insurance agent to make sure.

The one "gotcha" is the *loss damage waiver* (LDW). If you wreck a rental car, car rental companies can bill you for "loss of use"—that is, possible rental revenues foregone because the car was out of service. Depending on the company, they may bill you for $50/day—more for an expensive car—for two or three weeks or more (and usually longer than really required to repair the vehicle). Your policy typically doesn't cover this; so the ten or fifteen dollars you might spend for a day of LDW coverage might be worth it, especially if you rent a fancy car.

Question 221: **My brother has a nice sports car and won't let me drive it. He has full coverage but insists that I can't drive it because I don't carry collision or comprehensive protection on my own junker. Is he right?**

Short answer: no. Standard auto insurance policies cover the car, not the driver. So if you drive the car *with his permission,* you are covered.

Question 222: **How much homeowner's insurance do I need, and what are the main cost factors?**

The rise in home values and recent fire, hurricane, and other disaster events have brought homeowner's insurance into the spotlight. Simultaneously rising cost and risk have been a double whammy to homeowners' rates.

Unlike auto policies, largely driven by liability cost, homeowner's policy costs are mainly driven by cost to repair or replace the home. Generally, you should insure for as much as you can since a major uninsured loss can really hurt your financial position. Since land can't really be destroyed, land value shouldn't be included in coverage. If the insurance company is reluctant to cover full value (and most are these days), standard contents and outbuildings coverage can help make up the difference. Make sure to get some form of replacement value coverage (insurance companies are also reluctant to write "full" replacement coverage these days) to help fight the effects of inflation and, importantly, updated building codes.

Skyrocketing costs have moved companies to offer very high deductibles—up to $5,000 per event. Such high deductibles can save 30 or 40 percent on the premium. Remember that homeowner's insurance is to protect what's likely your biggest asset, not to cover small losses.

Question 223: **How can I save on my homeowner's insurance?**

With annual premiums rising to $1,000 and more for many homeowners, this insurance has become a real budget-buster for many individuals and families. The problem is exacerbated by increasing reluctance of major companies to write policies, especially in risky fire- or storm-prone areas. Rates vary widely across the country; so your location is important.

Assuming you've decided to stay where you are, the deductible is the biggest lever you can pull. By raising the deductible to $500, $1,000, $2,000, or even $5,000, you accept the small losses while covering the big ones and can save up to 30 or 40 percent on premiums. Put differently, $300 to $400/year in extra premiums is a lot to cover $5,000 in potential loss. You should also look at buying your auto policy from the same insurer. Insurance companies make more money on auto than homeowner's and may offer attractive discounts for the package deal.

Question 224: **I recently broke an expensive picture window, causing $1,000 in damage. I have a $500 deductible homeowner's insurance policy. Should I file the claim?**

Generally, "no." You stand to save $500 today, but today most insurance companies, unless forbidden by state regulations, are charging more to higher risk homeowners. Until recently, claims history had no impact on premiums for insurance already in force. But recently, to deal with escalating costs, insurance companies have changed homeowner's policies to act more like auto coverage, where claims can enter into each year's rating. (Many policies still exempt natural events such as wind damage from such increases, and you may also have special glass coverage—check with your agent.) The event on your record will make it harder to change companies, at least for the next three years. Go over it carefully with your agent before filing.

Question 225: **Do I need renter's insurance?**

Particularly if you're renting an apartment or condominium, renter's insurance is cheap and affordable protection. Not only does it cover loss of your own contents by theft, fire, flood, etc., but it also protects against damage you might cause to others. If you accidentally start a fire in your apartment, you may be liable for damages—even smoke damage—to other units and to the complex itself. For this protection, the price is attractive, even if you have nothing but particleboard shelves and a twenty-year-old TV yourself.

Question 226: Should I buy all of my insurance from one company or through one insurance agent?

By law in most states, insurance companies specialize in either property/casualty or life/disability insurance products. Because of its specialized nature, health insurance is usually written by specialist companies. So you can't usually buy all insurance from one company. Agents, however, are another matter. Agents can either be exclusive or "captive," that is, tied to a specific umbrella brand of insurance like State Farm, Allstate, or Farmers, or they can sell and service multiple lines of insurance. So you can usually buy life, disability, and property (but not health) insurance through a single agent.

Should you buy from one agent? There are compelling arguments to do so. First, you develop a relationship; they can understand your entire financial picture and recommend accordingly. Some offer discounts for buying auto, homeowner's, and life insurance from the same agent and body of companies. Realize, however, that some companies use one insurance line (like life) to subsidize another, so you might be better off buying simple term life from a life specialist or from the Internet. It's a tradeoff between cost and service, and the complexity of insurance may make service more important.

Chapter **13**

CONCERNING
INCOME TAXES

O f those two "sure things"—death and taxes—people probably get more worked up about taxes. For some people, taxes
are the clearest manifestation of mysterious and overbearing
governments; for others, they are just a necessary and terribly time-
consuming evil. A recent study found that Americans collectively
spend over 600 billion hours each year preparing tax returns. Beyond
time and effort, the subject of taxes conjures a lot of emotion, and
misconceptions and poor decision-making are widespread.

Many ask if they should do their own taxes. It's hard work and
tedious arithmetic for some. But besides saving preparer fees, there is
an important benefit: Preparing taxes can make you more aware of
your financial position. If preparation is left to others, it's still important to understand the process and result. There are legitimate ways to
save on taxes, while others only create illusions, like incurring a dollar
of unnecessary interest expense just to save 30 cents by deducting
it. People shouldn't jump at attractive-sounding tax strategies but
shouldn't be so afraid as to avoid them, either. The entire topic can't
be covered here, but the following questions address common misper-
ceptions and will help balance your view of taxes.

Question 227: **I am afraid of the IRS and reluctant to prepare my own taxes. Am I getting worked up over nothing?**

There are many others like you. With that said, a few words about taxpayer responsibility are in order.

Egged on by rumor and dark journalism, the IRS has been pasted with a "big brother" image, ready to pounce and punish the slightest mistake with the tact of a schoolyard bully. There may be a few incidents that fit this portrayal, but the vast majority of taxpayers are left alone. In reality, taxpayers are responsible for determining their own taxable income, and they are given some latitude to fairly determine and pay taxes on it. The IRS supports and even promotes *tax avoidance,* that is, the reduction of taxes through legal means. What the IRS does not tolerate is *tax evasion,* that is, where taxes are knowingly and unlawfully underpaid. The IRS will apply certain tests to see if deductions are reasonable and that income is recorded correctly. Through the letter and audit process, they will single out some returns and ask a few questions. If you made an honest mistake or have reason to do what you did, the IRS typically resolves quickly, efficiently, and in a friendly way, usually by phone and without penalty or lasting recourse. This may not convince you to do your own taxes, but the fear of ending up in jail for making a mistake is completely overblown.

Question 228: **What records do I need to keep for my taxes? For how long?**

Generally, the IRS has the right to detailed review of your past three years' taxes, so you need to keep all records of income and expenses at least this long. If you have a history of tax problems, IRS limits expand, and you should keep all records. For long-term transactions such as buying a house or securities investments, records should be kept indefinitely. At some point, you'll have to determine *basis* in the asset, that is, purchase price plus all additional expenditures for home improvements and other value-add items.

Question 229: **What are the basic steps to doing my own taxes?**

Doing your own taxes not only saves preparation fees, but also makes you more aware of your own finances—a big step toward financial success.

The first thing you need to do—important whether you prepare your own taxes or not—is organize income and expenses. If all income is from an employer, tracking income is relatively easy. You'll need an expense file for potentially deductible expenses like medical, interest costs, other taxes, and an assortment of other expenses. You'll also need to track investment activity and business and rental property interests.

Doing your own taxes involves, first, calculating your income and making some adjustments to arrive at *adjusted gross income* (AGI). Wages and salaries, investment income and others are added, and IRA and some other "for AGI" expenses are netted out. Second, determine *taxable income* by deducting either a *standard deduction* or *itemized expenses* and an *exemption amount for dependents*. The third step calculates tax on the taxable income, and the fourth step compares the taxable amount to what you've already paid in to determine a net refund or payment amount.

Admittedly, this sounds simpler than it works out in practice, especially if you have business interests or rental properties. But the basic process is the same and isn't that scary for most people, especially if organized.

Question 230: **My coworkers urged me not to go for a promotion and raise because I might end up in a higher tax bracket. Is this thinking right?**

In a word, "no." It is true that you might end up paying relatively more tax on the new income as compared to your previous income, but you will still come out ahead. Even if you move from the 25 percent to the 28 percent federal bracket, you still keep 72 percent of your additional income. It might be less depending on state income taxes, but by no means will you end up with less money or anywhere close. Perhaps your coworkers are just jealous.

Question 231: **Friends and family say I should get a bigger mortgage on my home to increase my income tax deductions. Is this thinking right?**

The answer to this question is similar to that of Question 230, only this time the issue is additional *deductible expenses* rather than additional income. True, most mortgage interest expense is deductible against income for tax purposes. But the most this deduction can save is your *marginal tax rate,* that is, the top tax rate corresponding to your level of reported income. The top tax rate for top income earners, that is, single or married persons earning more than $311,950 (2003), is 35 percent, and the most you can save by spending a dollar on interest is 35 cents. Most people—those in lower tax brackets—save 15, 25, or 28 cents and maybe a little more if state income taxes are included. Sure, if you have to get a mortgage to buy a house, the interest deduction is nice but don't go out and pay dollars in interest just to get cents of tax savings. It just doesn't make "cents."

Question 232: **What's the difference between a tax deduction and a tax credit?**

A *tax deduction* is an amount you can deduct from your taxable income before applying a tax rate, while a *tax credit* is a direct reduction of the amount you owe. Translation: a tax deduction will save you an amount determined by your top tax rate; if you're in the 25 percent bracket and deduct $1,000 in qualifying interest expense, you'll save $250. On the other hand, a $1,000 tax credit is a direct reduction in your taxes, and you'll save $1,000. Common deductions include mortgage interest expense, property, state and local income taxes, charitable contributions, and medical expenses exceeding a certain amount. Common credits include the all-important child credit available to most people under an income threshold (in addition to the dependent exemption). Other credits are available for child care, adoption, and certain educational expenses, to certain elderly or disabled people, and to some low-income people with children. A *nonrefundable credit* can only reduce tax liability to zero; a *refundable credit* allows tax liability to go below zero, meaning the IRS writes a check to you.

Question 233: **I am an employed social worker and use my in-home office to do paperwork and arrange client appointments. Can I write off any portion of my in-home office? How much?**

While the IRS has generally relaxed the rules allowing individuals to write off a portion of their home for business expenses, the qualifying tests are still strict, especially for employees with a business office provided. First, the portion of the home used must be exclusive and used regularly for your business; you can't write off part of your living room just because you do paperwork on your favorite couch. Next, is a tougher test for employed individuals: is the home "any one" of the following: (1) your principal place of business, or (2) a place where you meet or work with patients or clients in the normal course of business, or (3) separate from your home and used in your primary trade? Given the preceding facts, you probably don't pass this test. The home office isn't your exclusive place of business, and you don't meet clients at home on a regular basis. Still, it's worth watching how IRS rules and your work habits evolve.

IRS publications give straightforward advice on such complex issues, and IRS Publication 587 covering this topic is no exception.

Question 234: **I want to start making birdfeeders in my garage and want to write off about $800 in tools and part of my garage. Can I do this?**

The IRS makes a careful distinction between activities engaged in to earn a profit as compared to activities defined as a hobby. If the IRS decides your business is a hobby, expense deductions are limited to the amount earned and reported from the hobby. If the activity is "conducted with the intent to earn a profit," expenses may be fully deductible. The IRS has nine specific tests to determine whether a business has "intent to earn a profit" or is only a hobby. The main one: does the activity produce a profit in three of five years, or is it likely to? That test is combined with other more personal factors. Is the business conducted in a businesslike manner? Does it take a lot of time and effort? Do you have substantial other income? Does personal pleasure or recreation play a big part?

So if making and marketing birdfeeders becomes a big part of your life and there's a good chance of earning the $800 plus direct material costs, you may have a legitimate business and Schedule C business expense. But beware that the activity might be a coal mine canary that serves to trigger an IRS audit.

Question 235: **What are some of the common—and commonly overlooked—ways to reduce income taxes?**

Here are some common practices:

1. *Maximize retirement savings plans.* The federal government effectively subsidizes retirement savings, directly through deductible IRAs and pretax 401(k) contributions or indirectly by allowing investment gains to appreciate without current taxation.

2. *Use pretax dollars* wherever possible. Many employed individuals can use *flexible spending plans* to pay medical costs (like dentist office visits, eyeglasses), dependent care, and some insurance premiums. Pretax dollars go 25 to 35 percent farther.

3. *Know what expenses to itemize.* Track all household expenses and know when you reach standard deduction limits. Many people fail to itemize legitimate expenses.

4. *Take advantage of new tax law.* Learn how to use child credits and lower tax rates for investment income to your advantage.

5. *Start a legitimate business.* There are tough tests for a legitimate business (see Question 234), but if you can build a good business, many related expenses for home, travel, etc. become eligible for deduction.

Question 236: **Did the Bush Administration tax laws of 2001–2003 really save me money? How and how much?**

Although the debate continues about effects on the economy and long-term public finances, the new tax breaks really do save money for the average American. Savings come in five major ways:

■ *Reduced tax rate and elimination of the "marriage penalty."* Top tax rates for average earners dropped 2 to 3 percent. A "married filing jointly" earner making $60,000 after deductions paid $8,626 in 2003 federal income taxes, down from $11,107 in 2000.

■ *Higher standard deduction.* For the majority of taxpayers who don't itemize, the standard deduction for the same family rose from $7,350 in 2000 to $9,500 in 2003, saving about $537 in taxes at a 25 percent rate.

■ *Lower rates on investment income.* Maximum capital gains and dividend tax rates dropped to 15 percent.

■ *Increased credits.* The increase of the child credit to $1,000 per child provided large and direct savings for most families.

■ *Retirement plan contributions increased* to $3,000 for most IRAs, $14,000 for 401(k) plans, and catch-up contributions for fifty-and-over taxpayers.

Arguably, dollar savings available to higher-income taxpayers are larger, but most taxpayers in middle and lower income ranges can save hundreds and even thousands of dollars under the new laws.

Question 237: **What is "AMT"? When do I need to worry about it?**

AMT is the Alternative Minimum Tax, which came into being many years ago to boost the taxation of very wealthy individuals using special tax shelters and "preference items" to legally avoid taxes. While the intentions were good, the rules haven't kept up with the times. Many ordinary earners now earn enough and spend enough on preference items to qualify for the additional tax. Families earning more than $150,000/year and deducting more than

$49,000 for personal exemptions, standard deductions, state and local tax payments, and student loan interest can feel the bite. Families living in coastal areas or big cities—with high incomes, housing costs, and local taxes—are particularly vulnerable. Fortunately, recent changes have raised the $49,000 threshold for 2005, but AMT is still catching far more taxpayers than its designers intended and adding a lot of tax planning complexity as well.

Question 238: What are some of the biggest income tax traps and how can I avoid them?

The phrase "tax traps" sounds more sinister than it really is. It sounds as if the IRS wants taxpayers to overlook items and get caught, but that's not the intent. The intent—of Congress, not the IRS—is to make certain benefits and privileges unavailable to taxpayers outside intended beneficiaries.

For example, Roth IRAs are great, but Congress didn't intend to give this long-term break to joint filers earning more than $160,000/year, so they set a *ceiling* above which those taxpayers are ineligible. Similarly, Congress didn't intend for everyone to deduct every medical expense but to only deduct them in real hardship cases and so set a *floor* of 7.5 percent of adjusted gross income below which such expenses aren't deductible. A similar floor of 2 percent exists for "miscellaneous itemized deductions," meaning that Congress doesn't want to hear about them unless they are significant. *Phaseouts* are the most common adjustments. With phaseouts, certain benefits such as the child tax credit or deductible IRAs are fully available below certain income levels. But the child tax credit starts to phase out above $110,000 in adjustable gross income until disappearing completely at $130,000. Finally, there are *cutbacks*, where the amount deducted for an expense is reduced above a certain income threshold. Itemized deductions are reduced 3 percent for taxpayers earning more than $139,500 in 2003.

Good tax planning, especially for higher earners, requires being aware of these little tax traps and the intentions behind them.

Question 239: **I've been thinking about moving to a different state, and I am considering taxes as a factor. Does it really make a difference?**

The short answer: "yes." Even federal income taxes, which by definition are national in scope, can be different. Why? Because the *basis*—the amount you're taxed on—will be different. If you move from a place with low wages and costs to one with high wages and costs, the effective tax rate will increase, and you'll likely pay a greater percentage of income in tax.

But the real difference is found in state and local taxes, which can vary from a total of 3.2 percent in Wyoming to almost 20 percent in several East Coast states (2003). Some states have a more progressive tax code, so you might see taxes really jump if you're a high earner and change little if you have modest income. California is an example. The reference book *Cities Ranked & Rated* (Wiley, 2004) by this author examines these differences in depth.

Question 240: **I own a small hairstyling salon. How should I legally set up the business to pay the lowest taxes?**

This is a difficult question requiring careful analysis of your situation. The size of the business and whether you have employees makes a big difference.

The choices are *sole proprietorship, partnership,* and *"S"* or *"C" corporation.* Your choice is governed by three major considerations: (1) desire for legal protection, (2) preferred method of receiving income and paying taxes, and (3) how you want to use the business to buy benefits and build a retirement plan. Corporate forms ("S" and "C") provide legal protection against liability for events that occur in the business. "S" corporations protect for liability but allow you to pass income through without paying tax at the corporate level. You pay at lower individual levels. "C" corporations allow you to keep income in the corporation and pay for benefits out of the corporation, resulting in relatively limited wages and dividends passed to you. However, "C" corporation profits are taxed, and funds you do pass on may be subject to double taxation. Corporations cost money to set up and have a number of legal requirements.

The math is complicated, and if employees are involved, employee benefits and retirement become a big consideration. You should look for an advisor or CPA among your clientele.

Chapter 14

YOUR FINANCIAL LEGACY

You may have thought *estate planning* was just for the very old and very rich. Most people confuse estate planning with *estate tax* planning. Indeed, estate *taxes* become important at death for high-net-worth individuals with over $1.5 million (2005). But estate planning covers a much wider set of issues. It is really about the ownership and transfer of property through life, through incapacitation, and at death. It is about making sure your assets are handled properly when you can't and about making sure all members of your family (or families, if remarried) are protected. In some sense, it is about control since an estate without a transfer plan is managed by the state and courts—a lengthy, expensive process often with undesirable outcomes. Without doubt, estate planning covers those scary what-ifs we don't like to think about and involves scary-sounding things like wills and trusts, but really, it is about peace of mind for you and your family.

Question 241: **We are in our thirties and healthy. Do we need estate planning?**

Older people and people with infirm health have the most obvious needs to plan their own future and the transfer of their property. But younger, healthy individuals shouldn't ignore proper planning for the future of loved ones around them. Families with children need to plan in case something happens to the parents, and it isn't just about property. Who will get custody of the children, and how will those children be supported? If one parent dies, how easily and quickly will assets transfer to the surviving spouse to continue to meet financial obligations? If there are children from a previous marriage, how will you make sure they eventually receive your assets? How will you prevent your ex-spouse, you ex-spouse's new spouse, or that new spouse's children from receiving your assets? You might get a headache just trying to follow this but imagine the headaches of your bereaved dealing with these issues in probate after your death.

Question 242: **My broker and bank both recommended setting up our accounts as "JTWROS"—Joint Tenancy with Right of Survivorship. Is this a good idea?**

JTWROS guarantees immediate transfer and access to jointly owned property at death. Otherwise, even if the spouse were the obvious beneficiary through will or law, assets would likely be frozen until transferred in probate. This is a lengthy process even in the simplest cases. JTWROS costs nothing and makes assets immediately accessible, important for those left behind to keep things going.

Question 243: **I am married with a three-year-old daughter. Do I really need a will?**

Hopefully, you would never need it. But what if you and your spouse meet your end in an accident? Who will be the custodian for your daughter? Where will your daughter grow up? What if you don't meet your end in the accident but become incapacitated and unable to conduct your finances? Who will take over? Most people understand that a will gives instructions for how to transfer assets upon death. But it also gives instructions as to who should take over managing what remains when you can't. Without a will, the state decides according to law, not according to anyone's wishes. Beyond a will, a trust might insure financial sustenance for your daughter in case your chosen custodian is a good parent but a bad financier. Fortunately, the chances of something happening to both parents at once are slim, but you never know.

Question 244: What is a living trust? How is it better than a will?

A *living trust* is a legal entity designed to own and manage a body of assets on your behalf. You are the trustmaker; each trust has a trustee, or custodian, and at least one beneficiary. The trustee can be you, a professional, or your financially savvy uncle—you decide. In fact, you can do anything you want with a trust—deciding what's in it, who manages it, and who gets what from it and when.

The trust owns the assets and continues to do so after death unless you instruct otherwise. The trust distributes assets and income produced from those assets according to your instructions. The trust effects transfer of your assets *without probate* and without a will. There are three main advantages of a trust over a will. First, assets are transferred without probate, saving time, effort, and probate cost. Second, the trust can be used to accomplish more complex financial wishes, like providing income for your children from a previous marriage for twenty years after your death. Third, trusts are a good way to choose professional management for your assets before and after death.

The downside of trusts is cost: it may cost $1,000 or more to set up a trust, and professional custody costs still more. In the absence of special financial needs, you may not need a trust. A will and some easily transferred assets through JTWROS ownership (see Question 242) will probably do. Avoid high-pressure trust sales pitches.

Question 245: **What's the difference between a "living" trust and other kinds of trusts? Do living trusts avoid estate taxes?**

A living trust is a *revocable* trust, meaning you can change it any time while still living. The assets in the trust still belong to you and are part of your estate because you haven't committed them to anybody permanently. Because there is no such commitment, living trusts do not avoid estate taxes—this is a popular myth. An *irrevocable* trust permanently commits assets to others; it can be used to remove assets from your estate, thus avoiding estate taxes for wealthy individuals if properly planned.

Question 246: **I am divorced and remarried. In the event of my death, I want to support my current spouse as long as he/she lives, but then have remaining assets revert to my children.**

With today's high divorce rates, this is a common estate planning issue, and a good example of how trusts can be set up to achieve your wishes. There is a special kind of trust known as a Qualified Terminable Interest Property (QTIP) trust used to handle this kind of situation. With a QTIP trust, you can set aside some assets to cover the needs of your current spouse usually by granting the spouse an *income interest,* that is, making them the beneficiary for the income generated by the trust. When the spouse dies, that interest terminates, and the trust *remainder* reverts to the secondary beneficiary, your children. You may or may not enable your spouse to access the assets, or *corpus,* of the trust during their lifetime.

Question 247: **How big does my estate have to be before estate taxes become an issue?**

After policies had remained constant for many years, recent tax legislation has made a big mark on estate taxation. Originally, estate taxes were designed to prevent wealthy families from becoming ever wealthier, redistributing some of their wealth to others. Estates over

$600,000 were subject to taxes at very high rates, up to 55 percent. For years, only a few people had estate tax planning issues. But in time, more families that one would not consider wealthy were getting caught in the tax. Families with homes or farms they had owned for many years and even generations were being forced to sell a principal family asset just to pay the tax—hardly the original intent. So the bar was raised to $1,000,000 in 2001 with gradual increases through 2009, until it goes away completely—for one year—in 2010. Congress was reluctant to exempt estates from taxation forever; so in 2011, the exemption reverts to $1,000,000, unless changed (considered likely) by then. The limits are, in detail, $1,500,000 in 2005, $2,000,000 for 2006–2008, $3,500,000 in 2009, no limit for 2010, and $1,000,000 for 2011 and beyond. If you think this makes estate tax planning more difficult, you're right—for those still affected.

Question 248: **What is the difference between estate taxes and gift taxes?**

Estate taxes occur on assets transferred at death, while *gift* taxes occur on assets transferred while living. For many years until 2001, the taxes worked in tandem—the same exclusion, $600,000, applied to both taxes together. That is, gifts made during life were added to the estate value at death to apply the exclusion and determine tax. In essence, you couldn't just give away your estate on your deathbed. The important exception: up to $11,000 worth of gifts can be given each year per individual, per recipient, exempt from taxes. So a pair of grandparents can give up to $44,000/year to their two grand-children (two givers, two recipients). Such planned gifts can, over time, transfer a lot of wealth tax free for wealthier families. Recent estate tax exclusion changes have not been followed by gift tax exclusions—the exclusion remains at $1,000,000 indefinitely (see Question 247 for estate tax exclusions). This has made estate tax planning much more complex, but annual $11,000 gifts are still a favorite estate planning tool.

Question 249: **I believe the more lenient estate tax rules will expire in 2010 and the exclusion will revert to $1 million. I have $1.5 million and a number of heirs, including grandchildren, and want to avoid estate taxes. What should I consider?**

Here are some of the more common estate tax planning tools used in this situation:

> *Marital trusts*—if married—allow *each partner* to use their $1 million exclusion, giving a $2 million total exclusion. Commonly called "A-B" trusts, the "B" trust is set up upon the death of the first partner to accept that partner's share of assets in lieu of the surviving partner. Typically, the "B" trust contains assets equal to the exclusion amount.

> *Annual gifting*—Each year, $11,000 can be given per donor, per recipient, tax free. Two grandparents giving to three children (or their trusts) can shield $500,000 in taxable assets in about seven-and-a-half years ($500,000/$66,000).

> *529 plan*—These college savings trusts allow accelerated gifting; up to $55,000 can be given per donor per recipient in the first year. Gifted amounts can be used for a wide range of educational purposes and technically remain under the legal control and ownership of the donor in case there is some unforeseen old-age need (a 10 percent penalty may apply).

There are a few more obscure and complex tools. For instance, money can be donated to charity and replaced in death by life insurance purchased for a special irrevocable trust. There are also ways to put a primary residence in trust to avoid taxation. These more complex strategies should be approached only through a competent estate attorney.

Question 250: **I want a sizable portion of my assets to go to charity. What are the best ways to do this?**

The answer assumes you want to continue to benefit from your assets while still living. Otherwise, you could simply donate them today, realizing income tax savings today and possible estate tax savings later.

Specialized irrevocable trusts, *charitable remainder trusts* being the most common, can achieve your objective. Charitable remainder trusts allow you to set an amount aside, receiving an annual payment to support your needs. The *remainder*—whatever is left after you die—goes to the charity. A Charitable Remainder Annuity Trust (CRAT) pays a predefined annuity each year for a set period or for life, leaving the remainder for charity. A Charitable Remainder Unitrust (CRUT) pays a fixed percentage of whatever is left in the trust each year. Projected remainder interests are deductible for income tax purposes, and assets and potential appreciation can be untaxed. The beneficiary charity may be made known or kept secret. There can be more than one charity.

INDEX OF QUESTIONS

Chapter 4: **Choosing and Using a Bank**

Chapter 5: **About Debt and Credit**

Chapter 6: **Making Big Purchases**

59: My family really wants a new $3,000 plasma TV. How should I evaluate whether I can afford it?

60: What are the alternatives to buying expensive, new stuff?

61: My friends always try to impress me with their purchases—boats, vacation homes, whatever. Should I be impressed?

62: Should I buy the extended warranty?

PART II **Planning for Lifetime Goals**

Chapter 7: **Buying a Home**

63: Everybody says buying a home brings a number of financial benefits. Are they right? Why?

64: What kind of house should I buy?

65: How do I tell if a home is overpriced?

66: How much house can I afford?

67: Can I buy or sell a home without a realtor?

68: Obviously the mortgage is a big factor. What kind should I get and why?

69: How big should my mortgage be?

70: Should I get a 30-year mortgage or something shorter?

71: Why are interest rates so important? Do they really make a difference?

72: What makes mortgage rates change, and what should I keep track of and why?

73: What are the real costs of owning a home?

74: What are closing costs, and how should they be paid?

75: When should I consider refinancing?

76: Should I consider paying off my mortgage early? Why or why not?

77: My friends tell me I should buy rental property. Is this good advice? What do I need to consider?

Chapter 8: **Planning for College**

78: How much do we need to save for college?

79: What are the main ways to finance college costs?

80: What are the best savings alternatives, and how do they work?

81: I've heard a lot about 529 plans. What are the key features and pros and cons?

82: How do I choose a state for our 529 savings plan?

83: What are the advantages and pitfalls of prepaid tuition plans?

84: What are the major forms of tax relief for college costs, and how can they help?

85: What are the different kinds of financial aid, and which is best?

86: How "poor" do we have to be to qualify for financial aid?

87: What's the downside of student loans?

88: Should I borrow against my home equity to finance college?

89: Given all the tools, what is the best strategy for meeting college needs?

Chapter 9: **Planning for Retirement**

114: What is a spousal IRA?

115: What is a Roth IRA, and how is it better than a traditional IRA?

116: Our combined family income exceeds $170,000. Can we and should we still contribute to an IRA?

117: Where should I keep and invest my IRA assets?

118: What kinds of investments can I use for an IRA, and which investments are best?

119: I am most comfortable with real estate investments. Do IRAs and other retirement plans allow direct real estate investments?

120: I am self-employed. What retirement plans are available, and how do I choose the best one?

121: Is there a time where I must withdraw from my IRAs? When, how much, and what taxes?

122: When do my Social Security benefits become taxable, and how much tax will I pay?

123: What happens if I prematurely withdraw from my IRA or 401(k)?

124: What are annuities, and how do they work?

125: How much annuity can you get for your money?

126: What are the pros and cons of annuities?

127: What are reverse mortgages, and how can I use them in retirement planning?

128: Can you summarize retirement planning and saving strategy?

129: Scenario: I am fifty and know I've put off saving for retirement. I just spent a lot on sending my children to school. My income is $85,000/year, but I only have $25,000 in retirement savings. I live in a $100,000 home with a $60,000 mortgage. What should I do?

130: Scenario: I am forty and really want to retire early. Can I? How? My assets are income $80,000, home $250,000, mortgage $175,000 at 7.5 percent, current savings $40,000, and retirement savings $60,000.

Chapter 10: **About Investing**

131: Why is investing so important in personal finance?

132: I have my savings in a bank. Is this investing?

133: Please give a summary of the major investment types I need to be familiar with.

134: What is the long-term track record for the major types of investments?

135: Are there good rules about how to allocate my investments among different types?

136: How actively involved can/should I be in managing my investments?

137: As an investor, it is obvious that I need to stay informed. What are the best basic information sources?

138: I am a beginning investor. Should I use a full-service broker?

139: How do I choose a discount broker?

140: What is the case for investing in individual stocks?

141: What is the case for bond investing?

142: What is the case for mutual fund investing?

PART III   **Keeping the Ship on Course:
Avoiding Financial Surprises**

Chapter 11: **Protecting Life and Health**

230: My coworkers urged me not to go for a promotion and raise because I might end up in a higher tax bracket. Is this thinking right?

231: Friends and family say I should get a bigger mortgage on my home to increase my income tax deductions. Is this thinking right?

232: What's the difference between a tax deduction and a tax credit?

233: I am an employed social worker and use my in-home office to do paperwork and arrange client appointments. Can I write off any portion of my in-home office? How much?

234: I want to start making birdfeeders in my garage and want to write off about $800 in tools and part of my garage. Can I do this?

235: What are some of the common—and commonly overlooked—ways to reduce income taxes?

236: Did the new Bush Administration tax laws of 2001–2003 really save me money? How and how much?

237: What is "AMT"? When do I need to worry about it?

238: What are some of the biggest income tax traps and how can I avoid them?

239: I've been thinking about moving to a different state, and I am considering taxes as a factor. Does it really make a difference?

240: I own a small hairstyling salon. How should I legally set up the business to pay the lowest taxes?

Chapter 14: **Your Financial Legacy**

241: We are in our thirties and healthy. Do we need estate planning?

242: My broker and bank both recommended setting up our accounts as "JTWROS"—Joint Tenancy with Right of Survivorship. Is this a good idea?

243: I am married with a three-year-old daughter. Do I really need a will?

244: What is a living trust? How is it better than a will?

245: What's the difference between a "living" trust and other kinds of trusts? Do living trusts avoid estate taxes?

246: I am divorced and remarried. In the event of my death, I want to support my current spouse as long as he/she lives, but then have remaining assets revert to my children.

247: How big does my estate have to be before estate taxes become an issue?

248: What is the difference between estate taxes and gift taxes?

249: I believe the more lenient estate tax rules will expire in 2010 and the exclusion will revert to $1 million. I have $1.5 million and a number of heirs, including grandchildren, and want to avoid estate taxes. What should I consider?

250: I want a sizable portion of my assets to go to charity. What are the best ways to do this?

INDEX